To my mum, because she told me I
should dedicate this book to her and
I always do what my mum tells me.

Published 2017 by Smashing Media AG, Freiburg, Germany.
ISBN: 978-3-945749-51-7

Cover created by Veerle Pieters.
Editing and proofreading: Owen Gregory.
Print layout: Markus Seyfferth.
eBook production: Cosima Mielke.
Typefaces used: Elena by Nicole Dotin
and Mija by Miguel Hernández.

User Experience Revolution was written by Paul Boag
and reviewed by Marko Dugonjić.

Table Of Contents

About The Author

Paul Boag is a leader in digital strategy and user experience design. He has been working with organisations such as The European Commission, Oxford University and Doctors Without Borders for over 20 years.

Through consultancy and training he helps organisations make better use of digital technologies. He helps them meet the needs of today's connected consumers.

Paul is also a well respected figure in the digital sector. Author of five books including Digital Adaptation and Client Centric Web Design. He also writes for industry publications including Smashing Magazine, Sitepoint and Net Magazine.

Finally, Paul speaks around the world on user experience design and digital transformation. Alongside speaking he also hosts the award winning user experience podcast over at boagworld.com.

Foreword

Change comes slowly. Often it feels like you are continually hitting a wall. Although the community's commitment to change and adapt new design workflows and UX strategies is growing, it can seem nearly impossible to keep one's motivation fueled to individually change things. There is no debate that the customer matters and their journeys are essential. Nearly everyone agrees that a sparkle of delight with a beautiful UX can connect the customer with a brand and bring in more profit for the company. However, few know how to improve already existing processes without breaking the predictability and comfort of daily routines.

This change is not for lack of interest, skill, or experience. It's generally due to the daunting, infinitely complicated, and painfully slow process that we imagine making significant changes in organizations would be — a journey in which one willingly wouldn't want to embark. However, making significant changes doesn't necessarily require big efforts; it's just a matter of moving in the right direction, slowly but steadily.

I hope you enjoy reading this book, and you find yourself able to successfully tackle problems of all sizes in your organization. Let the journey begin!

— *Vitaly Friedman*

Getting Real About User Experience Design

Wake up, Neo. The Matrix has you.

The words that confirmed to Neo what he had always sensed. That nagging feeling in the back of his mind. The sense that something wasn't right.

If you're passionate about the experience of your users, you may feel the same. The belief that your organisation's culture is wrong somehow. That it doesn't reflect the real world your users live in. That your organisation must wake up and realise it is living in a delusion.

This book will help you start a revolution – a revolution that will jolt your colleagues and management out of their slumber. But to do this, you must follow me down the rabbit hole. You will discover yourself in a strange new world. A world in which you will not be comfortable.

Like Neo, you are about to discover just how deep the rabbit hole goes.

A world of business-speak, change management and economics. A world where an investment in a design-centric company would generate 228% greater return[1] than the same investment elsewhere.

Like Neo, you will need to learn new skills, overcome the system and open people's eyes. But enough of this overstretched analogy. Let's look at the reality.

Empower The Connected Consumer

It was a Tuesday morning and I was exhausted after catching an early train to get into London for a 9am start. I was meeting with a large financial services company whose mission statement at the time read:

1 http://smashed.by/ux1

Changing the way our customers feel about insurance through outstanding customer service."

If anybody was to understand the importance of user experience, it was these guys.

The meeting was to discuss a new online app their digital team had been developing for their latest product. Things started well with their lead user experience designer giving us a tour of the prototype he had built. Let's call him Dan. (I have changed the names in all my examples to protect the innocent and stop myself getting into trouble!)

Dan was in his mid-thirties with the wire-framed glasses that seem to be the staple of designers everywhere. His presentation was excellent and it was obvious he had done his homework. But as his presentation came to an end, he seemed to brace himself for a confrontation. At first I couldn't understand why. After all, he had tested the prototype with users and the business appeared to be dedicated to creating a great user experience.

Unfortunately, within moments of finishing his presentation I understood his apprehension. Janice from compliance was the first to speak up. "We will need to add some fields to the application form to follow regulatory requirements." I winced as I considered the impact of this on the average user. But this was just the beginning.

There were comments from IT about security, marketing about user data, and legal about terms and conditions. Before long, Dan's prototype was in tatters.

Worst of all, Dan didn't raise any objections. Instead he just took copious notes and went away to make the changes.

I spoke to him after the meeting and asked what had happened. He sighed, pushed his glasses up and rubbed his eyes. "That's normal," he replied. "Everybody says they want to offer a great customer service. But they're so busy covering their own arses that the user gets forgotten." "Why don't you push back?" I asked. "After all, you're the user experience designer. Isn't it your job to defend the experience of users?"

He looked at me with a mixture of defensiveness and resignation before replying, "I don't know anything about that other stuff. I'm a designer. Nobody would listen to me anyway."

In that short conversation everything became clear. I could now see why their mission statement wasn't translated into action.

Their user experience designers weren't user experience designers at all. They were user interface designers. They spent their days implementing interfaces.

They didn't see it as their job to tackle the bigger issues that harm the user experience.

The words of respected designer Mike Monteiro came to mind:

Walt Disney created user experiences. You create user interfaces."

This wasn't their fault. This was the constraint placed on them by the business. A constraint they felt unable to break free from. They weren't allowed to look at the wider experience like Walt Disney did. Even today, Disney is great at considering the entire experience, from your first visit to the Disneyland website all the way through to your hotel experience in the park.

But even if Dan were freed from these constraints, the structure and culture of the organisation prevented him from putting the user first. Each department had its own goals and objectives. Objectives that had little to do with crafting a great user experience. Objectives driven by their own targets and how management assessed their effectiveness.

If Dan's company was to survive in the modern world, things would have to change. The same is true for your company. Gone are the days when companies could get away with offering a substandard experience, where pumping money into advertising could cover a multitude of sins.

The world has changed and there is a new generation of empowered, connected consumers – consumers with higher expectations than ever before. If your company does not meet those expectations customers will go elsewhere. In fact, according to Customer Think, 89% of customers will stop doing business with a company after a single poor customer experience.

At its heart, that is what user experience design is all about. It is not about designing pretty interfaces or creating compelling brands. It is about better serving today's connected consumers. It is about recognising the power they now wield and ensuring you offer them outstanding service. It is about serving and not selling. And to do that, companies need to redefine their relationships with their customers.

Redefine The Customer Relationship

People who know me know I like to moan about my sleep. I feel like I have a constant battle to get enough sleep. I have tried everything from soothing music to drugs. Nothing seems to help.

But there is one thing that provides at least a little relief. It is a meditation app called Pzizz.[2] A combination of gentle music, guided meditation and isochronic tones which lull you to sleep. It isn't perfect, but it's a hell of a lot better than anything else I have tried.

2 http://smashed.by/ux2

Pzizz is working with its customers to improve the product.

Pzizz has a dedicated fan base of which I am a member. Unfortunately, years back they sold the app and the new owners abandoned it. But recently the original creators bought it back and they're rebuilding it from scratch.

Without the big budgets for advertising that some apps have these days, they have taken a different approach. They are trying to re-engage their core fans, those users who have stuck with them since the beginning. They are giving these people early access to the rebuilt app. Pzizz also seeks their opinions on everything from the new logo design to what voice to use for the guided meditation.

Judging by what Rockwell Shah, the man behind Pzizz, told me, it proved a smart move. Not only is their core audience excited about the product again, it is also helping improve the product itself. What is more, because we are contributing to the future direction of the product, we feel a sense of ownership. That makes us much more likely to recommend the app to friends. Heck, I am even writing about it in this book!

Pzizz is an example of a new generation of companies that are engaging with their customers to help shape products and services.

Involving customers isn't limited to Silicon Valley start-ups and app developers. Andrew Welch, chief executive officer of Y&R, suggests that over 50% of Fortune 500 companies[3] have made co-creation an integral part of their innovation strategy. This kind of co-creation is even being used in the construction industry. Hestatt and Von Hippel ran a three-day workshop together with its customers. In that time they came up with a new concept at half the cost of the traditional approach. Best of all, they had the new approach operational in only nine months, compared to the normal sixteen.

When many companies talk about engagement they are really talking about getting users to take action. But true engagement is much deeper than that. True engagement is

3 http://smashed.by/ux3

about listening to your users and allowing them to reshape what it is you deliver on a fundamental level.

UNDERSTAND AND RESPOND TO USERS' NEEDS

LoveHoney sells sex toys. The market has had a seedy reputation, earned in part by relying on explicit imagery to sell its products.

Lovehoney has been able to disrupt and dominate the sex toy market through outstanding customer service.

Lovehoney took a different approach. Rather than just those who had traditionally purchased sex toys, the company decided to go after a mass market: people who considered their sexuality a more private matter; people who would be uncomfortable with more traditional branding and marketing. Lovehoney dumped the explicit images and repositioned themselves as the "sexual happiness people."

But the company didn't just adopt a more accessible brand. It also changed the entire customer experience. It thought through the customer journey and changed their offering to enhance that experience.

Take privacy, for example. Lovehoney understood that its audience didn't want the world knowing they had bought a sex toy. It responded by changing how the sale appeared on a credit card statement. They also changed how they packaged and shipped products. There was no sign of the source, and the packaging had extra padding to ensure nobody would know what it contained.

But it didn't stop there. Lovehoney also knew that many people would be unsure about making their first purchase. They wouldn't be confident they had purchased the right product for them. That is why the company took the bold step of offering a 365-day unconditional return policy. You could buy a product and return it up to a year later, no questions asked. You could even return a product you had used! This relentless focus on providing the best buying experience has led Lovehoney to become the biggest retailer of sex toys in the UK.[4]

4 http://smashed.by/ux4

It has also enabled them to push into foreign markets.[5] It has given them unprecedented PR including their own TV documentary series, which focuses on their customer services team.

You may think that writing about a sex toy company is an unusual choice for a book like this. It is unlikely to be a case study you present to your boss. But I choose it with good reason. Lovehoney sold a sensitive product with high barriers to entry. Yet by allowing the customer's needs to shape their offering, it was able to redefine and dominate the sector. The user experience differentiated them.

Lovehoney is not alone in offering a fear-free shopping experience. For years, retailers claimed you couldn't sell shoes online. They believed customers would be too concerned the shoes wouldn't fit. But Zappos proved them wrong by offering a 365-day unconditional return policy just like Lovehoney. A return policy that gave customers the confidence to buy. Yes, some people abused that offer. But the increase in sales more than offset the losses.

Unfortunately, it only takes one part of the organisation to be pulling in a different direction for the whole thing to fall apart.

5 http://smashed.by/ux5

Work Across Silos

Creating a great user experience is more than a single person's job. We often talk about user experience designers as if this one person is responsible for the role. But in truth, creating a great user experience is only possible if the entire organisation works together.

Think for a minute about all the people who influence the experience at Lovehoney. There are the obvious digital professionals: the designers, developers, copywriters, marketers, data analysts, and so on.

But even though they are web-based, there are many other non-digital staff that have to create a great experience too. There are managers, customer support staff, finance people, warehouse packers, compliance people. The list could go on. Each person needs to consider the impact of their work on customers if the company wants to create an outstanding experience.

The structure of our organisations, however, can undermine this kind of joined-up thinking. Take a recent experience I had with my cellular network provider.

ENSURE COMMUNICATION ACROSS SILOS

I had bought a new iPad with cellular connectivity. Unfortunately, I was unable to share that connectivity with other devices using a personal hotspot.

I checked my cellular network provider's website and struggled to navigate its bloated offering. In the end, I gave up, finding no reference to my problem whatsoever. I resorted to calling the support line, only to sit on hold for over thirty minutes waiting to speak to a representative.

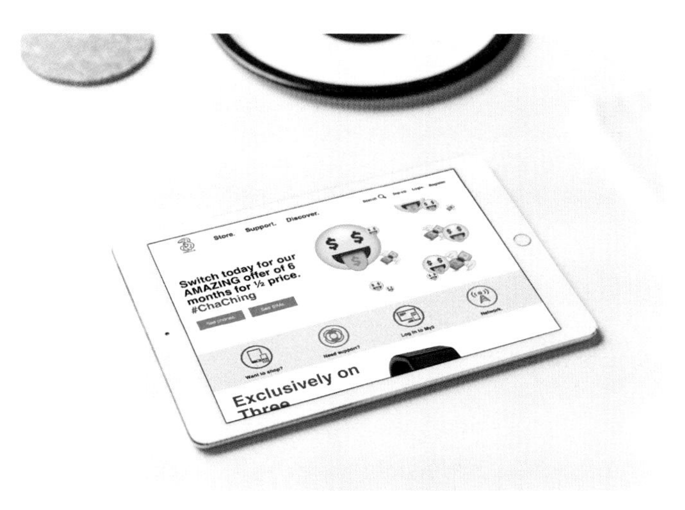

My cellular network provider's website was more concerned with selling me a phone than answering my question.

When I did finally get through to a human being, they were next to useless. It seemed to me they had no more access to information than I had via the website. The call ended with them suggesting I speak to Apple.

The contrast when speaking to Apple was striking. They answered my call promptly and immediately offered to replace the iPad. That said, they didn't believe the problem was with the iPad and I tended to agree with them.

Unsure what to do, I did what many consumers do these days: I ranted on Twitter. Almost immediately, I got a response from my cellular network provider's social media team. Not only did they respond quickly, they also had an answer to my problem and were able to fix it in minutes.

Did I go away happy? Not at all! I was angry and frustrated. I had wasted my time sitting on hold and trawling through a website when they had the answer all the time!

The problem was a lack of collaboration and communication between departmental silos. The social media team had not shared the solution with the call centre or the web team.

This siloed mentality seems to be near universal across almost all sectors. It is also becoming dangerous as creating a joined-up customer experience becomes more important.

In his book Silos, Politics and Turf Wars, Patrick Lencioni writes:

Silos – and the turf wars they enable – devastate organizations. They waste resources, kill productivity, and jeopardize the achievement of goals."

This is a common occurrence Universities are a great example. Their faculties are so siloed they compete against each other for prospective students. I have seen this lead to choice paralysis, where those same students end up going elsewhere.

I have seen digital services go hugely over budget because IT and marketing cannot work together. I have seen effort replicated, because departments don't communicate. All to the extent that it has damaged the company financially and in reputation.

In some senses this is not surprising. A compartmentalised business is much easier to manage. Each team has its own targets and areas of responsibility. Everybody knows where they stand.

When business silos fail to talk to one another the result is a bad experience for users.

As my iPad story shows, the user experience spans many departments. The typical customer journey will interact with marketing, sales, finance, delivery and customer support.

Procurement, IT, legal, compliance and many others also influence the experience. In fact, I struggle to think of a part of the organisation which has no impact on the experience of customers.

HOW TO START COLLABORATING ACROSS SILOS

Later in this book we will explore ways of collaborating across silos, but for now I want to point out the need for this kind of collaboration and encourage you to start interacting with other teams.

Start by understanding what it is these teams do and what they care about. Take the time to shadow colleagues in other departments. Spend a day with them as they do their jobs and ask lots of questions.

If you cannot find the time to do that, arrange meetings with each department and just get them talking about their role. People like it when others take interest in their job and so it is a great opportunity to build relationships. Relationships which will be invaluable when it comes time to raise the profile of the user within your company.

This might be the first step outside of your comfort zone. You might not find it easy talking to others. I have two pieces of advice for you.

First, you don't need to meet with the big bosses of the other departments. Seek out and engage with people at the same level as you. You will find it less intimidating and those people will appreciate the interest a lot more.

Second, preparation will help a lot. If you go to those meetings with a set of questions things will go much smoother and be a lot less awkward. Questions such as:

- Without referring to your job title, can you describe what you do?
- What about your department? What do its responsibilities cover?
- What does a typical day look like for you?
- What is the biggest headache you face in your job?
- What do you most love about your job?
- What contact, if any, do you have with customers?
- Are there any ways I could help make your job better?

Don't feel you need to stick to the questions above. At this stage, the idea is simply to strike up a dialogue with other departments, so the questions you choose don't matter that much. It is the contact that matters.

Once you have had these initial meetings, try to keep in contact with the people you meet. The best way to do this is ask for their opinion. For example, if you are working on a checkout process for a website, give your contact in finance a call. If you are working on frequently asked questions, make sure you have a chat with the person you met from customer support.

By building these ongoing relationships you will begin to address the gaps between silos that users can fall into. It will be a small beginning, but it is a start.

Focus On The Gaps

One thing my problem with a cellular network provider shows is that the user's experience is not a one-off interaction: it involves a series of touchpoints with your organisation. For example, I interacted with the website, the customer support team and social media within a few hours.

The number of touchpoints the average company has is increasing all the time. From mobile apps to new social channels, there is more complexity and more opportunity for things to go wrong.

Users interact with different departments, using different channels, on different devices. With this complexity comes the risk that users will fall into the gaps. I fell into an organisational gap when my cellular network provider's departments failed to communicate with one another. But I could also have fallen into a gap in the use of channels or devices. Take using a mobile device. How many times have you gone to a website on a mobile device only to switch to a PC because the experience was too hard? Rarely is that a seamless transition. Often you have to begin the entire process from scratch.

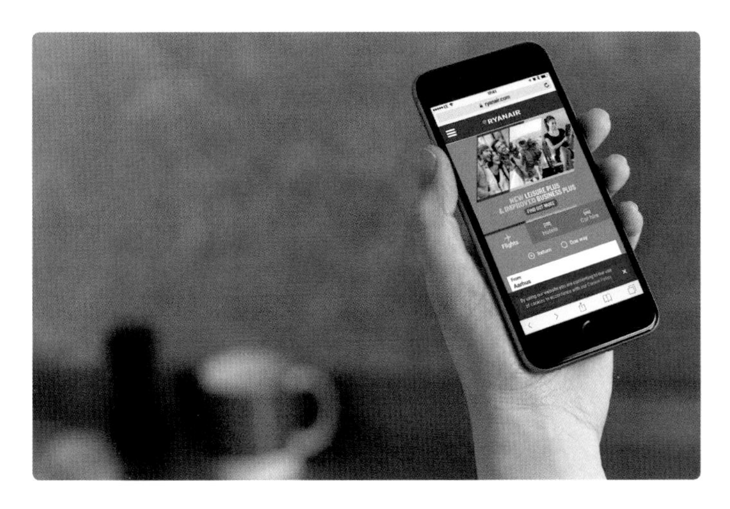

It is common to switch between devices especially when an interaction becomes difficult on a mobile device.

Moments like this are a real danger, points where you can lose the user because it is easier to go elsewhere. And this is a problem that will only increase as mobile devices proliferate.

But users do not just fall into the gaps between devices. They also can get lost as they transition between channels. A user might begin their interaction with you via social media before moving to a website or mobile app.

Once again, this is a danger, a moment where we can let the user down and alienate them. This might be a web page a social media representative pointed you at that failed to answer your question; or a website that encourages you to follow a Twitter stream for useful tips and tricks, but the account only delivers an endless stream of pointless press releases.

The point here is to understand that the customer experience is a journey. We need to smooth out the transitions along that journey, ensuring the user keeps moving forward.

CREATE SEAMLESS TRANSITIONS

How about banking? A typical scenario has you log in to your bank on a mobile device to check your statement. While looking through your transactions, you spot one you don't recognise. You need help identifying whether it is a legitimate transaction or not, so you pick up the phone and call your bank.

When the banking call centre answers, they have to verify your identity before being able to answer your question. But why? You just identified yourself when you logged in to the bank's mobile app. Why do you need to identify yourself again? The problem is that the two systems do not speak to each other.

Barclays bank in the UK does an excellent job at moving the user between channels.

Barclay's bank in the UK has addressed this problem. It has created a seamless transition between its mobile app and speaking to them on the phone. Once logged into the app, you will find a "Call us" button. On pressing this button the app calls the bank using your mobile phone, but instead of needing to identify yourself again, the app passes your data across to the call centre.

This might seem like a little thing but once you have experienced it any other banking app seems inferior. This attention to the user experience and those gaps in the journey help to set Barclays apart from the competition.

It understands the relationship between the online and offline experiences, that customers can be using a digital touchpoint one moment and a traditional one (such as a customer support line) the next. This is where it becomes important for us to understand the relationship between customers and users.

A User Is A Connected Customer

User experience design is a subset of customer experience design. Users are customers who are engaging with you via digital channels. So user experience design focuses on the experience customers have using those digital channels.

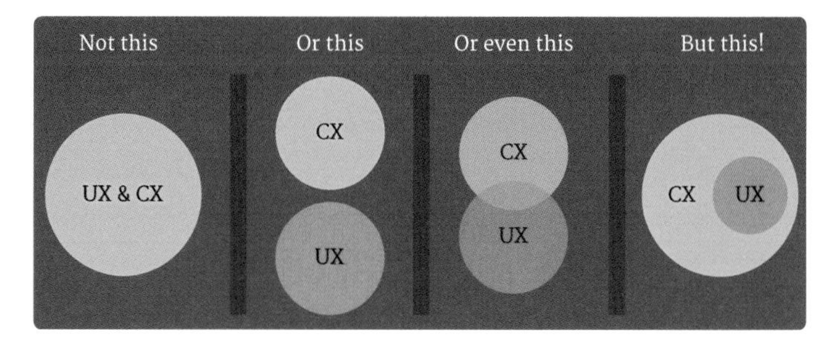

User experience is a subset of the overall customer experience.

The distinction between the two is not black and white. The line is becoming more blurry. Consumers use digital services in stores. Digital services are increasingly relying on offline elements like picking systems to deliver a better experience online.

The trouble is, many of us talk a lot about the user and little about the customer. This is part of the reason why our colleagues seem uninterested. By talking about users, we are framing the conversation as being about digital. But digital is a subject that is out of the comfort zone of many. Furthermore, colleagues often won't have a clear picture of a user in their minds, while they will have a better view of the customer.

In short, we need to be careful of the terminology we use. It will be much easier to find colleagues interested in improving the experience of customers than users.

Also, if we want to improve the user experience we need to consider the context. That means we need to think about the entire customer journey, not just the digital parts.

Design For The Journey

It is important to encourage your colleagues and managers to think of the customer journey. Without that point of view they will not see the issues of structure, culture and policies. Helping colleagues consider the user's journey is an underlying theme of this book. One tool that will start to open people's eyes is a customer journey map.

CREATE A CUSTOMER JOURNEY MAP

A customer journey map is a visual representation of the user's journey with your organisation. We can divide that journey into the different stages the user might pass through. For example, when purchasing a new car the journey might be:

- **Discovery**. This is the moment the user realises they want or need to buy a new car.
- **Research**. This is when the user starts to explore their options. What kind of car do they want to buy and what are their options for buying it?
- **Purchase**. The user decides to make a purchase. Interactions at this stage are crucial.
- **Aftersales**. The user will continue to interact with the dealer following a sale. They will need to get the car serviced and access other occasional support.

What the stages are will depend on your business. By having a series of stages you start to show colleagues that the user's experience changes over time.

For each stage you can explore the experience of the user at that particular moment. A customer journey map often contains the following information for each stage:

- **Tasks**. What is the user trying to do?
- **Questions**. What does the user want to know?
- **Emotions**. How does the user feel about the experience?
- **Touchpoints**. What parts of the organisation is the user interacting with?
- **Weaknesses**. In which areas is the organisation letting down the user?

The whole thing is important, but the last two areas are particularly useful in stimulating conversation with colleagues. It is also helpful for identifying gaps in the experience, moments in time where you let the user down.

Most of all, a customer journey map can be an invaluable tool for getting colleagues to consider the needs of users in their day-to-day work. At least, that is the idea in principle. In practice, you can spend a lot of time working up a customer journey map only for colleagues to consign it to a drawer. How then can you ensure your customer journey map gets people thinking?

RUN A CUSTOMER JOURNEY MAPPING WORKSHOP

The first thing to do is include colleagues in its creation by running a customer journey mapping workshop. This is an opportunity to bring together colleagues from across your organisation and a chance to get them discussing the needs of the user. The process of creating the map will in itself begin to change their attitudes.

There are two types of people that you should invite to a customer journey mapping workshop. There are those who understand the customer journey, and those who do not but are key influencers in the organisation.

It is often senior management who fall into the latter category. The more senior you are, the less you have to do with customers – yet the more your decisions have an impact on their experience. That is why these people need to attend a customer journey workshop. It helps focus them on customer needs and shows them the consequences of some of their decisions.

That only works if you also have people who understand the customer journey in the meeting. The most obvious source of these people is customer service, those who engage with users on a daily basis. They will have invaluable anecdotes of failures in user experience, stories you can incorporate into a customer journey map.

There are also other people with a contribution to make. Marketers often have insights into user behaviour based on market research they have carried out. Digital teams also have good contributions to offer, based on usability testing and analysis of web analytics.

Make sure that when these people attend the meeting they bring any research or data on users they have. If they have a lot of information, encourage them to summarise it down to a cheat sheet that you distribute to everybody at the start of the meeting. That said, the more material you have to work with, the easier the session will be and the less reliant it will be on personal opinion.

Once you have the right people in the room things should be straightforward. It becomes a matter of working through each stage. Identify what tasks and questions the user has, how they feel, and which touchpoints they interact with. Finally, look at your existing processes and identify any weaknesses.

	Discovery	Research	Purchase	Delivery	After sales
Tasks					
Questions					
Touchpoints					
Emotions					
Weaknesses					

Create a grid outlining the stages in the user's journey and the information you wish to gather on each stage.

You can do this by drawing a large grid on the wall with stages across the top and areas of interest down the side. Then use Post-it notes to fill in each cell with related questions, tasks, emotions, touchpoints and weaknesses.

Start by doing the first stage in the journey (discovery) together. After that, if time is tight, split attendees into groups and let each group address a separate stage in the journey. Try to avoid more than six people per group. Progress will slow otherwise. At the end you can come back together to discuss.

Customer journey mapping takes time. It will take the best part of three hours to map one possible customer journey. I recommend focusing on a typical journey for your primary audience. Remember, it is the act of exploring the journey that matters. It doesn't need to be perfect. The aim at this stage is just to get colleagues thinking about user needs.

KEEP YOUR CUSTOMER JOURNEY MAP IN PEOPLE'S MINDS

The danger is that after the workshop your customer journey map gets forgotten and shoved in a drawer somewhere. You can avoid this by turning it into an attractive infographic.

There is no right way of doing this, but it is often some kind of graphical timeline. I have also seen customer journey maps represented as a storyboard or even a video.

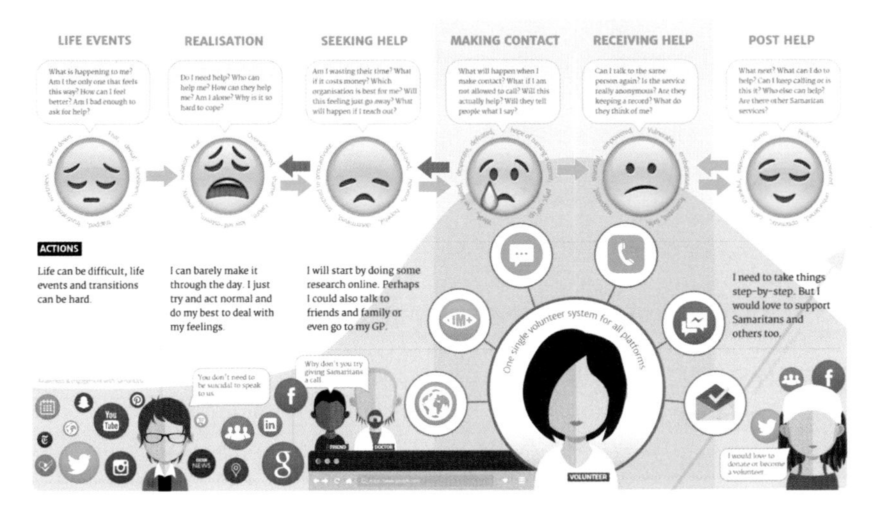

By turning a customer journey map into an attractive infographic it is less likely to be ignored.

My personal favourite is to turn a customer journey map into a poster that you can put up on the walls around the organisation. Whenever your colleagues look up from their desks, they will be reminded of the user's experience.

Too many organisations cover their walls with awards, or photos of executives or their own products. This screams that the organisation is inward-looking. What about replacing those photos with the user's experience? Maybe this could be the beginning of our journey of raising the profile of the user within the organisation.

A customer journey mapping workshop and infographic are great ways of engaging with colleagues. But it is important to remember that it's superficial. It is not going to transform the organisation and it will not even be that representative of the user's actual experience. For that, we will need to delve deeper.

Delve Deeper With Your Research

I am often shocked how little organisations know about their users. Instead of real information, they operate on assumptions and data that are out of date.

The exception to this is marketing. They tend to have a deeper insight. You might find they have personas that break down the demographics of their users. Unfortunately, marketing's focus is on customer acquisition. Data extends little beyond the initial phases of the journey. Also, knowing that a user drives a BMW or reads the Guardian isn't that useful from a user experience perspective. Personas contain information designed for a different purpose.

Although these personas by MailChimp are great reminders to staff to focus on the user, they don't say much about what the person wants to do.

Yes, we care about who and what influences customer thinking, but we need more. As is clear from the customer journey map, we care about their questions, tasks and feelings.

The problem is, we often lack time to do this kind of research. But if we don't make time for it, we are never going to convince anybody of anything. Without user stories and hard data, how are our colleagues going to begin to understand users? And if they cannot picture users and their needs, how can we expect them to consider those users in their decision-making?

The only way we are going to build a user experience culture in our organisations is if we can paint a vivid picture of the user in their minds. But to do that, we also need to know the user intimately. Can you honestly say that you do?

SPEND TIME WITH USERS

It was a Friday and I wanted nothing more than the weekend to arrive. But before that, I had a day of field testing ahead. This was the first time I had ever decided to meet with users in their homes, rather than in usability labs. I say decided, but it wasn't my choice. The client had suggested it and I couldn't say no. Little did I know it would be the most eye-opening experience of my professional career.

The users I met that day were in their seventies. I knew a lot about them already. I understood they had accessibility issues due to poor eyesight and arthritis. I knew they took their time using a website and lacked confidence (judging by the analytics). In fact, I had built up a solid view of their behaviour. But the moment I started meeting them in their homes, I realised how little I really knew.

I met Roger who had fought in the Battle of Britain. I met Jill whose disabilities left her housebound, and Peggy who owned more cats than any one human should. Suddenly these users turned into people. People with names, faces and life experiences. People I wanted to fight for and create better experiences for.

If you are going to be a champion for user experience in your organisation. If you are going to convince others of the importance of putting users first, you need to meet them in person. Not in some sterile usability lab, but in their homes. You need to get to know them, see where they live and understand their lives. You need to hear their stories and experiences.

Not only will this change you, it will also give you invaluable stories to tell. Because stories are powerful.

LEARN TO TELL COMPELLING STORIES

Don't get me wrong, data matters. A lot. We need data on conversions, bounce rates and dropouts. We need to be able to quote levels of engagement, search terms and more. But that is not enough by itself. We need human stories too.

If you want to change the behaviour of your colleagues and motivate management, you need to do more than quote figures. You need to be able to show video of users struggling, share their experiences and quote what they have to say.

I have sat in management meetings and showed stats on dropout rates from the website with no results. They weren't willing to invest in fixing a theoretical problem based on data that was open to interpretation.

But then I would show them a video of users struggling with the website. Users getting angry and frustrated. Users saying they would never use the site again, or complaining that they couldn't read the tiny text. This completely changed attitudes.

Don't misunderstand me. You cannot have anecdotal stories without data: the two go hand in hand. Together they build up a compelling and detailed picture of the user that will get people to take notice. A picture that will make people care about the user.

If we want to bring about change in our organisations that is what we need to do. We need to get colleagues and management to care. To do that we need to become better at selling the benefits of user experience design.

How To Sell The Benefits Of User Experience Design

Michael was in his mid-fifties and the dean of a faculty at a large UK university. With grey hair, a deep Welsh accent and a look of intense concentration, he exuded academic authority.

We were discussing the copy on his faculty website. I was suggesting we needed to rewrite it to make the content more accessible. The reading level was high and it was full of jargon. I knew that a simple rewrite could improve the user experience.

But Michael seemed unconcerned with the problem. He argued that they weren't interested in students who struggled to understand the copy. As far as he was concerned, they were not bright enough for the institution.

User experience didn't appear on Michael's agenda. In fairness to him, he is not alone. Most academics in universities care little about the student experience. They see their role as researchers and academics, not as service providers to students. They are more concerned with securing the next round of funding and their own career progression.

This may sound like I have a negative opinion of Michael, but that is not the case. I like him a lot and he is a smart man. But he is the product of his career. And like humans everywhere, he is more concerned with his short-term personal goals. He isn't as interested in longer term, organisational objectives.

I see this time and again. Not just in academia, but across all sectors. Executives are more concerned with their agendas than fulfilling the needs of users. This makes convincing them of the value of user experience design very hard.

Even user experience expert Jared Spool struggles to persuade executives to care about user experience.

User experience expert Jared Spool summed it up brilliantly in his article "Why I can't convince executives to invest in UX (and neither can you)."[6] The answer doesn't lie in convincing them about user experience. Instead it lies in appealing to self-interest.

One way to achieve this is to demonstrate a threat to the status quo.

Understand Customer Expectations

Put yourself in Michael's shoes for a moment. His university has been around for hundreds of years. Every year since he took his post, he has been turning students away. Students weren't his problem. He was more concerned with his academic status and the reputation of the faculty.

Why should he spend time solving something that, in his eyes, wasn't broken? If his copy has been good enough for years of students, why isn't it good enough now?

This is a common and understandable reaction. Why is this important? It has been fine for years. After all, there are two things people don't like: unnecessary work, and change. Unfortunately, user experience design often requires both.

6 http://smashed.by/ux6

The problem with Michael's perspective is that it is out of date. His world is static. The university has remained unchanged for generations. He sees no reason to do things differently now. But the world is changing all around Michael and I failed to communicate that. Student expectations are changing and the university would have to adapt or lose its status, lose that surplus of students every year.

Finding evidence to support this belief isn't hard either. A quick Google search shows the stagnant rate of university applicants in the UK[7] and increased competition for international students.[8] We really have no excuse for failing to put together compelling arguments when we have the whole of human knowledge at our fingertips!

A big part of the change in academia is that students in the UK now see themselves as consumers. With a shift from grants to student loans and tuition fees, the cost of higher education has skyrocketed and so students have become much more demanding. They expect a great user experience.

But the change is deeper than that. It is a change that affects almost every sector. Digital has changed consumer behaviour. For a start, it has given us unprecedented choice.

7 http://smashed.by/ux7
8 http://smashed.by/ux8

USERS HAVE GREATER CHOICE

I know I don't look old enough, but I went to university before the web was around. I narrowed my selection of possible universities on the basis of printed prospectuses. This limited me to about ten universities. Of that ten, I visited three and applied to two.

Today, students can find out detailed information on almost any university on the planet, all with a quick search. They have extensive choice and are no longer constrained by personal network or geography. All the choice in the world is just a Google search away.

Users have all the choice in the world, just a Google search away.

So it is with almost all sectors. Once, a customer's personal network and a company's advertising reach limited choice. Now, choice is at everybody's fingertips. You are no longer competing locally – often you are competing globally.

This is a profound shift in the fundamentals of business. Most consumers face a wealth of suppliers. Supply now outstrips demand.

So much choice affects customer behaviour. Customers can be overwhelmed by choice. This means they spend less time evaluating each option and their tolerance for problems plummets.

USERS HAVE LIMITED TIME AND TOLERANCE

In western society, time has become one of our most valuable commodities. We are busy, stressed, and have little patience. Faced with an overwhelming amount of choice we use the slightest imperfection to narrow the field.

My wife was kind enough to prove this point recently. It was a rainy Friday afternoon when in the middle of a laundry load our washing machine gave up.

After much grumbling and some colourful language, she concluded that we needed a new washing machine. She had enough on her plate, and she wasn't keen on the idea of having to deal with this too. Her loving husband made himself scarce for fear she would give him the job.

Later I checked in with her as she was trawling through sites looking for a good replacement. “I don’t have time for this,” she grumbled. She dismissed many washing machines based on one or two bad reviews and a mental checklist of requirements.

When she did settle on a new washing machine, she started the process of deciding where to buy it online. There was no way she was going to a physical store for something she cared so little about.

After searching based on price, she settled on a site and went to make the purchase. But the checkout process seemed to be one hurdle after another. It wouldn’t accept the password she used. It rejected her credit card because she formatted it in the wrong way, and it didn’t return our house on postcode lookup.

With an overwhelming amount of choice, consumers become increasingly fussy.

In the end she exclaimed, “Right. That is it. I am going to buy it from Amazon. I know how that site works.” She ended up paying more, but to her mind she had spent too much time on the other site as it was. It was time to get the job done and move on. She had no patience for a frustrating website.

That is the reality we live in. Yet many businesses fail to grasp this fact. They make excuses.

Your management team might do the same. They might argue their business is different and so this example does not apply. They might say that their customers are local and so that narrows the field. They might even suggest your sector has little competition and so user experience doesn't matter.

They are, of course, right. There will always be a weakness in any data or story you present. Even if you do your research online, gathering data and case studies, they are not going to be about your company. Your situation will be unique.

But this is often a distraction technique. Management don't want to face the issue and so they pick holes in your evidence. That is understandable, because accepting you are right means they need to act. That is tough.

The response is a simple one. Don't argue. Instead, agree that your research has holes. Suggest that the company needs to do its own research. Speak to users, run surveys, analyse the competition and gather data about their situation.

This doesn't mean that gathering case studies and data about other companies isn't important. Sure, management might dismiss these as irrelevant, but it will plant a seed of doubt, enough to justify investing some of your time in talking to your own customers.

Because even if your boss is right, it does not change the fact that digital has altered customer attitudes. They are less tolerant, more time-sensitive and have higher expectations.

USERS HAVE HIGHER EXPECTATIONS

You see, you are no longer in competition just with your competitors. You are in competition with the whole web.

Let's return to the university. The students it is trying to reach use services such as Twitter, Facebook, Google and many others every day: digital services they can use completely free of charge.

Not only are these services free, but they are also built with the user experience in mind. They are easy to use and offer extensive functionality.

It is not surprising that students find the digital tools built by universities frustrating. They are inferior to the likes of Facebook and yet students pay huge amounts of money in tuition fees every year.

Your management team might suggest that this is an unfair comparison. How is a university meant to compete with the investment made by Google, Facebook or Twitter? If you are a smaller business the challenge is even bigger.

They are right: it is unfair. But it is what consumers have come to expect, at least on a subconscious level. No matter your sector, customers are no longer just comparing you to your competition. They are comparing you to every great user experience they have enjoyed.

Even if this is not the case, expectations are still rising. Philip Tellis summed up this rise in expectations nicely[9]:

What delighted users a few years ago is now an expected baseline, the absence of which will frustrate."

In fact, 76% of users[10] expect web applications to have improved over the the last three years. Part of the reason for this is that there has been a fundamental shift in power.

THE BALANCE OF POWER HAS SHIFTED

In the pre-digital world, the power lay in the hands of the company. They had the budget to reach a mass market. They had the reach to push their products and their agenda. They had a voice.

Today, that power dynamic is shifting. Part of the reason is the choice consumers have now. With choice comes power. Power to choose somebody other than your company. Power to negotiate. Power to expect more.

9 http://smashed.by/ux9
10 http://smashed.by/ux10

But that isn't the whole story. There is another factor at play here: consumers have a voice.

Let me ask you a question. How many people follow you on Facebook or Twitter? I mean you, not your company. The average Facebook user has 338 friends.[11] That is an impressive number of people who value your opinion. Add to that the viral effect when one of your friends shares one of your updates with their own network. In that context, the average consumer has a big reach.

Now think about what you do when you look at a product on Amazon. What do you do first? Do you read the manufacturer's description or do you skip straight to the reviews? Well, 70% of consumers take action[12] based on a customer review. We trust the opinion of complete strangers, often even over the company that produces the product or service.

This shift cannot be overemphasised. If you provide a bad user experience to even one customer, the consequences can be enormous.

Take the story of Hasan Syed. British Airways lost his father's luggage. As Hasan struggled to retrieve the luggage, he became frustrated. In the end he decided to pay for a promoted tweet. Any time somebody mentioned British Airways they saw the following tweet:

11 http://smashed.by/ux11
12 http://smashed.by/ux12

Don't fly @BritishAirways. Their customer service is horrendous."

Within hours, the tech blog Mashable featured the story. Mainstream media followed shortly after. All because British Airways failed to provide a good user experience.

MashableUK
Business
Man Buys Promoted Tweet to Complain About British Airways
20.1k SHARES
Share on Facebook
Share on Twitter
In a world where airlines lose your luggage, one man couldn't stand it anymore.
No, this isn't a movie. In a real-life instance of the little guy challenging a giant corporation, Twitter user Hasan Syed has taken on British Airways by buying a promoted tweet to complain about his father's lost luggage.
BY TODD WASSERMAN
SEE ALSO: What the World's Biggest Websites Looked Like at Launch
What's Hot
Indian gay couple celebrates their love in candid photo shoot
713 SHARES
Did you notice the tiny, significant change to the 'Game of Thrones' opening credits?
1.7K SHARES
Google will launch its own phone this year, report says
957 SHARES

A single customer can cause a major PR headache for even the largest of companies.

That is the power of the web and the reality of our modern world. It is this reality that we need to share with our colleagues and management. We need to be unafraid to expose our organisations to the uncomfortable reality they now live in. Like Neo, we need to help those in the Matrix wake up.

But scaring people is not enough. Like a rabbit trapped in the headlights of a car, a management team can be paralysed, unsure how to respond. We need to show them a better way.

Share The Successes Of Others

Focusing on the threats can be a good tactic, but it is not enough on its own. You also need to outline the opportunities. This is especially important for companies keen to grab market share. A commitment to user experience offers unprecedented opportunities to disrupt a sector. A chance to challenge the established players. This is a pattern we have seen again and again.

Uber began because two friends were complaining about the annoyances they had to deal with in their lives. One of those annoyances was catching a cab.

If you think about it, catching a taxi is far from straightforward. Before you even try and hail a taxi you need to make sure you have cash on you. Too often they only take cash even when they advertise that they accept cards.

Hailing the taxi isn't easy, and if you are in a foreign country communication can be hard. Not to mention the feeling that they may well rip you off by taking you on a longer route. Finally, once you reach your destination there is that scrabble to pay and get a receipt, all while parked with traffic piling up behind you.

Uber addresses all these issues in the user experience and more. Hail a cab via the mobile app and pay automatically on a registered credit card (including tip). Track the route on a map and get a receipt emailed when you arrive. The whole process is streamlined.

By making use of modern digital tools Uber has been able to offer a superior experience. One that strikes fear into any cab company when Uber arrives in their city.

Uber has threatened many existing taxi companies, causing strikes and complaints of unfair competition.

Since its launch in 2010, Uber has provided over 1 billion rides to 8 million users[13] in 400 cities. It is valued at over

13 http://smashed.by/ux13

$50 billion[14] by providing the same service as any other taxi company but with a focus on user experience.

Another example of a company disrupting a sector is Airbnb. The service that allows people to rent out rooms or apartments has redefined the hotel industry. Depending on who you ask, Airbnb is currently valued anywhere between $10 billion and $22.5 billion.[15]

Airbnb had a slow start, particularly in New York, one of the key locations it was targeting. The founders of the company decided to book out 24 spaces in the city to find out what the problem was. It turned out that the user experience was the problem. As one of the founders put it:

The photos were really bad. People were using camera phones and taking Craigslist-quality pictures. Surprise! No one was booking because you couldn't see what you were paying for."

The company decided to take a big gamble. They decided to pay for every property to be professionally photographed. It paid off big time.[16]

The host experience improved dramatically. They were over the moon to get professionally taken photos of

14 http://smashed.by/ux14
15 http://smashed.by/ux15
16 http://smashed.by/ux16

their property. Users got a better experience too as it was much easier to see what they were getting.

Most of all, these improvements in the experience paid off for Airbnb too. Sales skyrocketed and the free photography attracted more hosts.

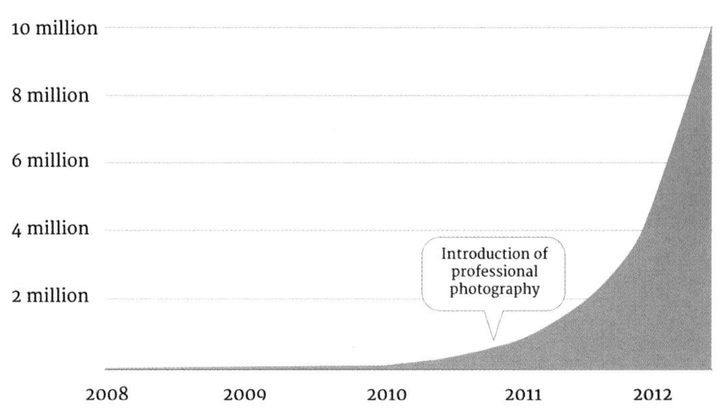

By investing in better photography, Airbnb was able to improve the user experience and dramatically increase bookings.

But a focus on user experience doesn't just allow you to disrupt a sector. It also allows you to sell products or services in ways impossible in the past.

For a long time people said it wasn't possible to sell shoes online. After all, you need to try on shoes. You have to be confident they'll fit. Many believed this was one area where a physical store would always win out.

Then along came Zappos with its outstanding commitment to customer experience. They offered a 365-day return policy and covered the postage. That meant people could order shoes with absolute confidence they could return them if they didn't fit. All at no cost to them.

Zappos was so successful that it was purchased by Amazon for $1.2 billion.[17]

The great thing about user experience is that it can benefit almost any sector. You don't have to be a Silicon Valley start-up.

NOT JUST FOR TRENDY START-UPS

In my last book, Digital Adaptation, I mentioned a company called Wiltshire Farm Foods, which sold ready meals to elderly people. Not exactly the typical home for outstanding user experience. But it was user experience that allowed them to compete with the big supermarket chains. After all, why else would somebody buy frozen ready meals from them when they could get the same from Tesco for less?

Wiltshire Farm Foods understands its audience. They know that elderly people feel vulnerable, and don't like delivery men coming to their homes. That is why they show a picture of your delivery man whenever you place an order

17 http://smashed.by/ux17

on their website. All delivery drivers are also police-checked for added reassurance.

But that is just the tip of the iceberg. They will unpack deliveries for customers. They will check up on them to make sure they are OK and even take repeat orders on the door with cash payments.

The point is that Wiltshire Farm Foods has used customer experience to set themselves apart in a crowded market. As a result it was able to increase its e-commerce sales by 10,000% in only five years.

USER EXPERIENCE IN THE B2B SECTOR

So far, all my examples have been business-to-consumer (B2C). Perhaps you work in the business-to-business (B2B) sector. I can imagine your management arguing user experience is not as important there. They would, of course, be wrong. If anything, the opposite is true. B2B products and services are more expensive and so customers feel more entitled to quality. Also, business customers are even busier and so less tolerant of mistakes.

But business customers are still people. A B2B customer is also a B2C customer much of the time. They see quality user experiences in their personal life and expect the same at work.

There are a huge number of B2B companies that are betting on user experience, the most notable of which is IBM. IBM is investing $100 million in expanding its user experience consultation services.[18] This involves opening ten interaction experience labs and hiring 1,000 new employees. As Bridget van Kralingen, senior vice-president of IBM Global Business Services, put it:

There's no longer any real distinction between business strategy and the design of the user experience. The last best experience that anyone has anywhere, becomes the minimum expectation for the experience they want everywhere."

And IBM is far from alone. From new players such as Salesforce[19] to companies like General Electric,[20] user experience is a rising star in B2B. This shouldn't be surprising. Whether B2B or B2C, user experience design brings significant organisational benefits.

Highlight The Organisational Benefits

Many seem to perceive providing a great user experience as a luxury their businesses cannot afford. To some extent this is our fault. We focus on the benefits user experience brings

18 http://smashed.by/ux18
19 http://smashed.by/ux19
20 http://smashed.by/ux20

to the user, when we should be focusing on the benefits it brings to the business.

A great user experience is not the cost of doing business. It provides enormous benefits that increase sales and lower costs. But before we look at those, let's take a moment to consider the brand benefits it provides.

USER EXPERIENCE BUILDS BRAND

Often the first group of people within a business to understand user experience are marketers.

Providing a good user experience makes a lot of sense from a marketing perspective. After all, every marketer knows that the holy grail of marketing is word-of-mouth recommendation.[21] If you can get your customers advocating your product or service it is more effective than any other form of advertising.

By providing a great user experience, customers are more likely to recommend you. I am sure you can think of times you have recommended a product or service to a friend. Often that is as much to do with the customer service you received as the actual product.

21 http://smashed.by/ux21

Superdry is just one brand that has replaced traditional marketing with word-of-mouth recommendation.

In the world of the connected consumer, customers aren't just recommending you to their friends. They are posting reviews and ratings, changing how complete strangers see your brand.

They are also sharing your business with their audiences and creating buzz around your brand. They are working hard on your behalf to increase your brand awareness.

When I wrote about the balance of power shifting, I wrote about the dangers of customers having their own audience.

But it provides amazing opportunities too. Your customers have become your greatest advocates and a great experience is how you mobilise them.

It is the experience that differentiates. In a global marketplace of competitors there will always be somebody who offers a comparable product. That means if you want to stand out, creating a great experience is the way to go.

This is especially important in well-established sectors. At first, just getting to market is enough: if your product or service is new people will buy it. Then it becomes about features. Do you offer more than the competition?

As the sector matures, more and more of your competitors will offer something similar. If you are to differentiate you need to innovate. But where do you go next?

You can, of course, innovate in the experience you provide. But that isn't all I am getting at here. Good user experience design works in collaboration with customers. It always engages with and learns from the user.

Your users are full of suggestions about how you could improve your products and services. If you just listen to them, the result will be better products and more sales.

Take Evernote, the note-taking software. It has built a community of advocates,[22] people who promote the product – and also influence the direction the product takes.

In the end, sales is what it is all about. If you want to promote user experience design in your business the key is proving it can provide more sales.

USER EXPERIENCE AND INCREASE SALES

The impact of user experience on the sales funnel cannot be over emphasised. There are countless stories of the profound impact of user experience design on sales. According to Software Engineering: A Practitioner's Approach by Roger Pressman, every dollar invested in user experience design returns anywhere between $2 and $100.

When American Eagle Outfitters focused on user experience, they increased their sales by 53.6%. By conducting user research, United Airlines increased online ticketing by 200%. There is no doubt that investing in user experience design has a direct impact on conversion. But it doesn't stop there.

According to Willy Lai, director of user experience and creative design at Samsung, user experience will also improve average order value.[23] If you make the lives of your users easier they will spend more with you. It is that simple.

22 http://smashed.by/ux22
23 http://smashed.by/ux23

They will also buy from you more often. Improvements in user experience will increase the number of repeat purchases. When Staples redesigned its website there was a 67% increase in the number of repeat customers.

When Staples improved the experience of its users there was a ***67% increase in repeat customers****.*

These benefits don't just apply to e-commerce sites. Sure, it is easier to track the benefits on an e-commerce site, but improving the user experience will benefit service-based businesses too.

Whether you are B2C or B2B, user-centric digital services will have a direct impact on sales. This is a message we need to get better at communicating to management.

The argument that user experience design can improve sales is compelling. And user experience doesn't just increase sales. It also improves profitability by helping make considerable cost savings.

USER EXPERIENCE COST SAVINGS

Spiralling costs are a constant concern to management teams. This will be one of the biggest barriers you will face when shifting your organisation to be more user-centric. You will find management resistant to hiring user experience experts to move the company forward. The last thing they want is an increase in operational costs.

Yet building a user experience culture can help to reduce those costs. We need to be able to explain that at the appropriate time to management.

For a start, many organisations face considerable customer churn. In other words, they are always having to find new customers. This is a time-consuming and expensive proposition. It means a significant investment in marketing to grab the attention of consumers. Then there is the cost of sale: persuading those consumers to buy. In short, losing customers is expensive.

Creating a great user experience will reduce this cost, because it will improve customer loyalty. More repeat customers means less marketing and a lower cost of sale.

If the customers you have are advocates, this further lowers marketing costs. The people they recommend you to need less persuading.

But user experience design can do more than lower the cost of sales and marketing. It can also lower other operational costs.

If customers are unhappy with their experience, you will see more complaints and returns. Dealing with these is an expensive business.

Even if customers are not dissatisfied, they often have questions. That is why organisations need customer service teams. Telephone support for these kinds of queries can be expensive. But what if a customer could get the answer themselves?

The UK government saved the tax payer over £2 billion a year by shifting 88%[24] of its interactions to digital self-service. They also are not alone. In fact, this has proven a constant in government reporting.[25]

Such savings are not limited to government. One mobile operator saved €5.75 million[26] by encouraging customers to rely on online support.

24 http://smashed.by/ux24
25 http://smashed.by/ux25
26 http://smashed.by/ux26

The GOV.UK website saved over £2 billion a year by shifting to a digital self-service model.

At first glance, incorporating user experience design into a typical project may appear to add time and cost. After all, talking to users takes time. But, in truth, it will save time and money. That is because you will design the right solution from the beginning, rather than having to adjust further down the line when the cost of change is more expensive.

When companies incorporate user experience design into projects, they test early using prototypes. This allows them to catch and fix problems through iterative usability testing and redesign.

It is far less expensive to make changes to a prototype in the early stages than it is later on. Forrester estimates[27] that for every $1 to fix a problem during design, it would cost $5 to fix the same problem during development. Even worse, if a problem is not spotted until after release that price rockets to $30.

What is more, you may find that you can completely avoid developing unnecessary functionality. Many projects make huge assumptions about what it is customers want or need. By testing with users early, you can establish whether those assumptions are correct; if they are not, you can avoid the cost of developing something nobody wanted in the first place.

Of course, I am preaching to the choir here. If you are reading this book you already know the benefits of user experience. But maybe I have helped clarify the arguments in your head so you can articulate them better.

Even with a compelling case, however, you are going to find it hard to convince management to change the way the company operates. Instead, we need to start the ball rolling without them. That means building a core group of user experience advocates. Your lone voice is not going to get the job done.

27 http://smashed.by/ux27

Create Customer Experience Evangelists

I first met Harry at an industry conference where I was speaking about user experience design. He came striding over to me after my presentation and announced to me in a broad Glaswegian accent that I was "talking bollocks."

It turned out that he didn't disagree with what I was saying, he just thought I was naive to think my suggestions would work in the real world.

"Sure, all this stuff is good in principle. But getting anybody to agree to it is nigh on impossible," he told me. "I have been banging on about user experience for years and nobody will listen to a word I say."

I found myself warming to Harry's no-nonsense character and we ended up sitting in the bar that night chatting.

Harry had been working in a large organisation (which will remain nameless) for most of his career. He had become passionate about user experience a few years back and started to bang the drum for it within the organisation.

He had spoken to management countless times. He had pointed out where they were letting the user down across the organisation. He had even outlined how the user experience could be better throughout the journey. Yet instead of his bosses encouraging his passion, he met constant rejection.

As I listened to Harry's story, I had to confess I wasn't surprised at what I was hearing. Although Harry was enthusiastic, he was going about it all wrong and alienating people along the way.

Harry saw himself as the sole custodian of the user experience, a lone maverick trying to bring about change single-handedly. The more he met resistance, the more he saw himself as the only one who cared. Over time, he ended up bitter and angry at his management team and colleagues. He came to see them as the enemy.

But maybe Harry was receiving pushback not because his colleagues had a problem with improving the experience of users. He received pushback because of the way he was going about things.

Although I loved Harry's direct nature, I imagine he came across as arrogant and that he gave the impression this was his area of expertise and others didn't have much to contribute. Of course, as I explained in chapter 1, this is not true.

No one person can design the user experience. It takes collaboration between many people across many business silos.

I suspect Harry's colleagues felt as if Harry was telling them how to do their jobs, and that he was invading their territory. That might not have been so bad if all Harry's suggestions were good ones. But he would have had a particular perspective on what the user experience could be, one shaped by his own expertise and background. There would have been a lot of elements he had failed to consider.

I assume colleagues and management saw Harry as an annoyance. A single voice, pushing his own agenda and causing unnecessary disruption.

I am sure you are not like Harry, but there is a chance your colleagues could see you in the same way. There is also a danger that you might become disheartened like Harry, and either become angry like him or just give up.

We cannot do this alone. We need others who care about this issue as much as we do. People who can help us champion the cause and encourage us when it gets tough; people who can stand alongside us as we talk to management.

More than that, we need our colleagues' expertise. We won't have all the answers. By ourselves, we cannot understand the entirety of the user experience, let alone how to fix it.

Our colleagues will have unique insights into aspects of the user experience we don't understand.

You might be a great designer, but you are probably not an expert in improving site performance, a key factor in the experience. You might be a great marketer who understands what the user thinks, but you will know little about point of sales or handling returns. It will take more than your expertise to create a great experience.

You will also not have all the answers about creating change within your organisation. Your colleagues will know who to talk to, how to present to management, and what to do to get things moving. The more of our colleagues we can get on board, the more momentum for change we will be able to build. We need the numbers and we need the expertise. Without those two things we will be dismissed as a lone wolf, somebody our colleagues will resist.

How, then, do we get our colleagues on board? Well, we start by finding those who already care about user experience.

Find Colleagues Who Care

I know what you're thinking. You are thinking that you are the only person who gets user experience within your organisation.

Maybe you are the only person who knows about usability testing, user interface design or user research. But that doesn't mean you are the only person who cares about the user having a great experience.

It is surprising just how many people in your organisation will care about customer experience. Calling them customer evangelists at this point might be a bit of a stretch. But they care about the customer's experience because a poor experience makes their job harder. Your job is to track these people down.

The most obvious starting point is marketing. A marketer's job is almost impossible these days if existing customers are not happy with their experience. Sales people will also care for similar reasons.

You will also find customer evangelists in other places. Customer support is a great place to look. These people deal with customer complaints every day. Fixing the customer experience will make their jobs much easier. Anybody who interacts with a customer often will be a potential evangelist.

Not that everybody cares about the customer experience because it has the potential to make their lives easier. There will also be those with professional pride. I encounter a lot of customer advocates within IT, even though they have little day-to-day contact with customers. They care because that is industry best practice. They see providing a great experience as part of their job.

Start by writing a list of people you know who might fall into some of the categories above. It doesn't need to be a big list. It might only be four or five people depending on the size of your business.

REACH OUT TO YOUR POTENTIAL EVANGELISTS

Once you have your list, I would recommend meeting each of them. Having lunch together is always my preferred approach because it is a more informal atmosphere to talk. If your list is a bit long for that, meet with people in small groups based on their discipline. If you have a couple of marketers on the list, meet them both together.

The idea of the meeting is not to push an agenda or ask them to do anything specific. Rather, it is an opportunity to express your concerns over how your company engages with customers and see if they feel the same.

Share your frustrations and the problems as you see them. Try to focus on the opportunities for creating a better experience. You can use some of the arguments in the previous chapter for inspiration.

Be careful not to say anything that people could see as a criticism. Try to keep the whole conversation upbeat and positive.

The most important thing to do is ask them questions.

- Do they have frustrations of their own?
- What would they do to improve the experience of customers if they had the time and money?
- What is the biggest complaint they hear from customers?
- What do they think is holding the organisation back from providing a better experience? What are the barriers to change?

Listen to what they say and take the comments on board. Reflect their thoughts back to them to show you have listened, and agree with them as often as you can.

As your time draws to a close, suggest it might be nice to form a small group of people who are keen to improve the experience of customers. Ask them if they would like to be a part of that. Also ask them who else they think should be in that group. If you know the people they suggest, make a note of who they are; if not, ask for an email introduction.

With any luck, by the end of the meeting they will be on board and have suggested some more names you can contact. Once you have repeated this process a handful of times you should have a group who share your concerns, a group with at least a nominal interest in change. You should also have a few more people to contact.

With these new people to contact, you have a couple of options. If you know them, it might be worth meeting with them just as above; if not, get an email introduction before following up yourself.

Writing an email like that can be tricky. Below is a sample email I wrote for a charity with a few thoughts on why I have written it in the way I did.

Hi Ann,
As you know I got your email address from John after a recent meeting we had to discuss the experience of our fundraisers.

Both I and John feel there is more we could be doing to improve the experience of our fundraisers. John suggested that you may feel the same and that I should drop you an email.

Start by making it clear why you are writing and who you are. In this case you are a contact of John's and you are writing about the experience of fundraisers.

In our conversation, we concluded that improvements to the fundraiser experience could increase donations. We also believe it has the potential to lower our support costs.

Outline some of the benefits you see from improving the experience of users.

We also felt that happier fundraisers would make them more likely to promote us online. As you are responsible for our marketing we thought this was particularly relevant to you.

Explain the benefits a better experience would have for the recipient. Show them how it would make their job easier.

We had a load of ideas in the meeting about things we could do but felt we could learn a lot from your contribution.

Show you value their contribution and opinions.

With that in mind, I am setting up a small discussion group to explore some possibilities. Is this something you would like to get involved in?

Make it clear what you want them to do.

Don't worry, it is all informal at this stage and won't involve a lot of work. You can just contribute as much or as little as you want. We are just keen to get your input and involve you in our thinking.

People don't like to commit themselves to more work or meetings. Make sure you make it clear that this wouldn't be an onerous task.

If you have any questions please let me know, otherwise just give me the nod and I'll add you to the group. We are excited about your involvement and hearing your ideas.

End by making them feel appreciated and emphasising you would value their contribution.

Don't get demoralised if you don't hear back from them straight away. Most people spend their days fire-fighting and as this isn't a high priority email it might get forgotten. If you don't hear back in a week give them a gentle nudge.

Once you have met some people and emailed others you will have a small group interested in improving the experience of customers. Now we need to decide what to do with them.

GET YOUR CUSTOMER EVANGELISTS TALKING

So far our little group of evangelists have only spoken to you. We need to get them speaking to each other. Until they start interacting together they are not a group.

Once they start talking they will reinforce each other's desire for a better customer experience. It will become more important to them as they start discussing it with like-minded people.

There are lots of options for getting the group talking together depending on how your company operates.

Some companies use a chat app like Yammer or Slack to communicate. These are great communication tools if people use them often. I have seen too many Yammer groups set up only to see them die because nobody is checking Yammer that much.

Another option is to have regular meetings, though most of us already have too many meetings in our diary. Coordinating calendars is a nightmare and will only become more challenging as the group grows.

Often the best approach is to create an email group. Most people live in email and reply regularly to communications in that way.

Chances are your company has an easy way of creating an email group using Outlook or Exchange. But if not, try something like Google Groups. Google Groups gives you one email address that sends to all recipients. It also allows you to search the archive which might be useful later.

Google Groups is a great way of managing a discussion between a small number of people using email.

Of course, the tool you use matters less than what you say. It is important at this stage to get the group enthused and sharing ideas. This will fall to you, so make sure you spend time encouraging discussion.

You want to keep the discussion positive. Ironically, a good way to encourage conversation is to get people to express their frustrations. People like a good moan and they find it easier to identify problems than come up with solutions.

With that in mind, ask the group to share their biggest customer experience frustrations. What is it that drives them nuts about the way the company interacts with customers?

Let them do that for a while before picking out a few of the frustrations expressed for more discussion. Ask people how the group would solve the problem if they could do things as they wanted to. Let that run for a while before asking what barriers would make implementing the idea difficult.

With luck, the conversation will start to flow. If people go off on tangents, let them. If they say things you disagree with, let it slide. Now is not the time to educate them about user experience best practice. The aim is to encourage discussion in the group. Anything that endangers that should be gently but firmly squashed.

The most common problem will be people saying that an idea wouldn't work. This is an important conversation to have, but people will become afraid to express ideas if they think somebody will shoot them down.

When people start to shoot down an idea, ask them to come up with a way of overcoming the barrier they have identified. If somebody says:

"There is no way you would get that by Jim in compliance."

Ask them what they would need to happen to get Jim on board. That way you keep the conversation positive and moving forward. This discussion will create a lot of positive ideas for change, but most of all it will unify the group behind the idea of improving the customer experience.

In the end, the conversation will begin to run out of steam as the ideas dry up and the barriers start to feel insurmountable. At this point you need to step back in and suggest the creation of a common vision for the group.

ESTABLISH A COMMON VISION

A handful of people talking about a better user experience might seem like a small beginning. You may feel like you haven't a hope of bringing about change. This feels especially true if you work in a large company. Yet that is not the case.

Change happens when people unite behind a cause. As more people latch on to that cause, it builds momentum. In the end, it will reach a tipping point and become unstoppable even when faced with sceptical management.

To gain that momentum you will need something for people to unite behind – a rallying point. Sometimes this is a person, but often it is an idea or set of values.

Everybody from world religions and political parties to self-help books and corporations use this approach.

The Government Digital Service took this approach to change the culture of the British government. While working on a website prototype, the team of sixteen people[28] put together design principles[29] as Post-it notes on the wall. These principles have become the pillars that define how the UK government builds digital services.

Many organisations around the world have copied this approach. From the US government's Digital Services Playbook[30] to Google. These manifestos for creating better user experiences have rallied staff behind a new way of thinking. Your small team of UX evangelists need to take the same approach if they want to grow into a movement for change in your organisation. What goes into a set of principles like this?

WHAT TO PUT INTO YOUR USER EXPERIENCE PRINCIPLES

The best way to think of a set of principles is as a manifesto for change. You are outlining what needs to happen to become a company driven by user experience. I am not talking about a strategy, but rather a list of characteristics

28 http://smashed.by/ux28
29 http://smashed.by/ux29
30 http://smashed.by/ux30

Your principles can become posters, videos or infographics. Anything that helps promote user experience best practice.

This will start as a document. In time it can become videos, posters or infographics, anything that can promote the principles around the company. Whatever form it takes it needs to be short and easy to understand. That includes the initial document.

A good place to start is with an initial statement outlining the need for change. This only needs to be a couple of paragraphs. What it contains will depend on your organisation. It might read something like this:

Today's customers have higher expectations than ever before. We need to deliver on these expectations if we are going to increase market share and outmanoeuvre our competition. To achieve this we need to rethink how we do business. We need to focus more on the needs of our customers. This is especially true when utilising digital channels where consumers are ever more demanding.

To this end we have produced a set of ten principles that we should seek to adopt as an organisation and embed into our culture.

With that in place you can start thinking about the principles themselves. Ten is a good number, but don't feel constrained by it. You may need more or fewer depending on the circumstances of your organisation.

Each principle should have a short description to explain it. But keep them concise. Nobody is going to read a lot of copy.

Below is a sample list to get you started.

Understand what people need.
If we are going to provide an outstanding experience to customers we must take the time to understand their needs. By understanding their needs we can ensure we provide the best experience. But we will also be able to build the right solution first time, so saving the organisation wasted resources.

Decide with data.
We make too many decisions by committee and conjecture. Instead of guessing what will work and what will not, we need to do the research that provides us with data to make decisions.

Focus on simplicity and clarity.
Using our services shouldn't be stressful or confusing – and yet it often is. Making things simple and clear takes work. We need to be willing to put in that work. This will involve making hard choices. We may have to drop products, services or functionality for the sake of simplicity.

Test and iterate.
The best way to ensure a great experience is to start with a minimal viable product and then test it. Learn from the results and then iterate before testing again. Through a cycle of iteration and testing we reduce risk by avoiding big failures. Instead, we will make small failures that we can learn from and correct.

Uniformity without conformity.
We must endeavour to create a uniform experience for people across all our products and services. We should use the same language and design patterns. This helps customers become familiar with using our services. However, this should not become a straitjacket. We will still need some variations to serve the needs of specific groups.

Start with people's needs, not specifications.
Too often projects begin with a list of proposed functionality or requirements. Instead, we must begin with the needs we are trying to fulfil for our customers. These needs should shape the project rather than us letting internal drivers define it.

Challenge constraints.
While endeavouring to meet the needs of consumers we will encounter organisational roadblocks, from IT policy and branding guidelines to compliance issues and financial policy. Instead of accepting these constraints we need to question them. Just because a constraint made sense in the past does not mean it does so now. The organisation needs to question whether the constraint is worth the cost to the user experience.

Consider the whole experience.
We cannot consider people's interaction with a single part of the experience in isolation. We also need to consider how it fits into the bigger picture. If we are designing a digital service such as a website, we need to ask how that fits alongside offline touchpoints too.

Launch is just the start.
Often projects end with the launch of a new product or service, but this should just be the beginning. Once a new product or service is publicly available we should watch how users interact with it. There should be time and resources available after launch to refine the offering based on what we discover.

Technology should follow experience.
Many digital projects begin with the procurement of a technological solution. The user experience is then constrained by what the technology can deliver. Instead, projects should begin by defining the user experience. We can then buy technology capable of delivering that experience.

Remember, this is not a definitive list. It is just an example to help you envision what a set of principles might look like. It falls to the group to discuss and decide on the final list.

DECIDE ON YOUR USER EXPERIENCE PRINCIPLES

How you decide on your list of user experience principles is important. Although it is tempting, you cannot just present a draft set of principles to the group for their approval. Doing so will not give them the sense of ownership over those principles that you need.

We need the group to feel they created the principles. If they do, they will be more likely to promote and defend those principles with colleagues. But allowing the group to shape the principles could be tough. You may feel you are best positioned to do the job. After all, you brought the group together and you have read this book.

They may make additions you don't agree with, or they may disagree with some of your suggestions. It is important that you set your ego aside and allow the principles to be a group creation.

One of the best ways to start is to show them some examples of other principles. There is my list above, as well as the UK and US government versions I have mentioned.

There are others: you can find a great collection at Design Principles FTW.[31] Not all the principles in this collection are orientated around user experience, but they should inspire some discussion among the group.

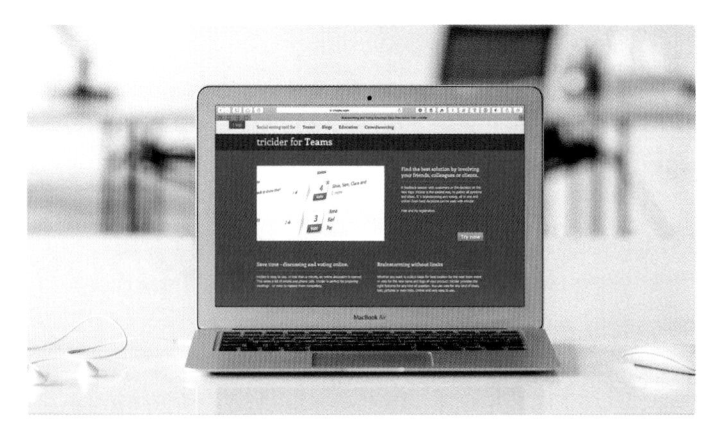

Tricider is a great tool for collaborating on principles and allowing the whole team to vote.

31 http://smashed.by/ux31

How you collaborate and decide on the principles is up to you. One option is to allow anybody in the group to suggest a principle. Other participants can then vote for that idea if they like it. Ideas with enough votes then get included in the final list. A tool like Tricider[32] is ideal for this job.

To begin with you will see a frenzy of activity, with lots of suggestions and discussion. But as the list begins to take shape you may notice conversation getting bogged down in details about wording and what should be in or out.
At this point it is important to remind the group that this isn't a fixed set of principles. They should evolve and change over time. This is just an initial starting point. Once others in the organisation get involved, the list will alter. Also, once you start using your principles, they may need to change. For the time being keep things fluid.

You will discover that the principles are an invaluable tool for engaging the rest of the company. This is something we will get into in the next chapter. But for now the main benefit is focusing the group and getting them working together.

The creation of your principles is the first step in wider collaboration between group members. Collaboration is the first step to creating a joined-up user experience.

32 http://smashed.by/ux32

Pool Your Knowledge Of The User

A good next step is to share knowledge about your audience. It is tempting to think that your organisation has no user research, but it is often surprising just how much information on customers is lurking about in office drawers.

As I said in chapter 1, marketing will have information on customers' preferences and demographics. Your web team will have access to analytics data and maybe even some usability test results. Customer support will know what questions people ask again and again. Sales will understand what motivates customers into action. Account managers will have great case studies and testimonials. The list could go on.

With your user experience principles in place, now is the time to start sharing what you know about your users. This will enable everybody to have a more complete picture of the people you are trying to reach. It is also a great way of getting everybody working together.

If you don't have something like an intranet or document repository, create one. I recommend something like Evernote, but even a password-protected blog or wiki would also do the trick.

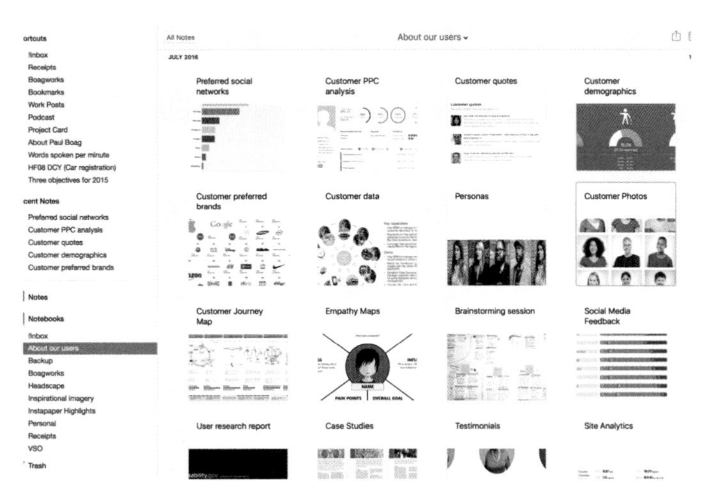

Create a single place where you bring together all you know about your customers.

At this stage we want to keep the amount we ask of people as small as possible. With that in mind, just ask people to copy and paste anything relating to the customer into your central resource. There is no need to smarten it up at this stage. We just want to make it accessible to everybody.

Once all you know about users is pulled together in one place, start rationalising it. One option is to start putting together a customer journey map like the one we discussed in chapter 2.

But let's hold off on that for a while. A customer journey map will take a greater time commitment from your evangelists and we don't want to overburden them. At the moment, it is all about keeping them excited and motivated. We can use a customer journey map later as a way of engaging with the wider company, as I will discuss in the next chapter.

Instead, let's start by asking the group to identify and prioritise the key audiences. Try to break the audiences down into five or six different groups. If you have a lot of audiences, just pick the five or six most important. If you feel you have fewer, no problem; look at whether you can break those audiences down into subsets.

Once you have a list of users prioritised on their value to the business, the next step is to define their needs a little better. Personas are one way of doing this – you may already have personas in your repository. Another useful tool to consider is an empathy map.

An empathy map is a picture of the customer focused on what they want to achieve. There are different versions of an empathy map but they all consist of six sections.

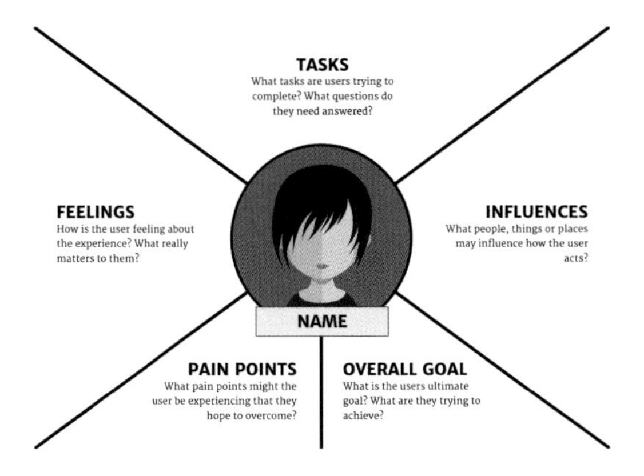

An empathy map is a picture of the customer focused on what they want to achieve.

My favourite configuration is:

- **Tasks.** What tasks are users trying to complete? What questions do they need answered?
- **Feelings.** How is the user feeling about the experience? What matters to them?
- **Influences.** What people, things or places may influence how the user acts?
- **Pain points.** What pain points might the user be experiencing that they hope to overcome?
- **Goals.** What is the user's ultimate goal? What are they trying to achieve?

Alongside personas, an empathy map builds a clear picture of the customer.

Start by drafting some initial empathy maps for the key audiences. Use the information in your repository to help with this job. Depending on the amount of information available to you, you might be making some pretty big assumptions, so be sure to pass the results by your user experience group for their feedback.

If your group is enthusiastic, spread the work by asking people in the group to each tackle an audience. They can then present the result to the group for discussion.

With your final set of empathy maps in place, consider turning them into posters. This will be useful as we attempt to raise the profile of the customer experience across the organisation.

We now have everything we need to start a company-wide campaign to raise the profile of user experience. We have:

- A set of benefits that user experience provides (as laid out in chapter 2).
- A team of people who care about the customer experience.

By turning an empathy map into a poster you keep the customer in the minds of colleagues.

- A set of principles so people understand what a culture focused on user experience would look like.
- A repository of information about our customers we can draw on.
- Some empathy maps to get people thinking about the customer.

Time to get to work.

Raise The Profile Of The Customer

Let's imagine two employees at two different companies. We'll call one Nigel and the other Helen. The companies have been around for the same length of time, are of similar size, and operate in the same industry.

Both Nigel and Helen work in legal. Their job is to make sure the companies meet their regulatory obligations and protect them from risk. Both are nice people whom you would enjoy an evening out with. But while Nigel is a constant roadblock to improving the experience of users, Helen is not.

Nigel wants users to agree to lengthy terms and conditions. Helen was willing to compromise on a version written in plain English.

Nigel demanded that a cookie notification appeared on every page of the website. Helen spent time with a designer coming up with the least obtrusive option possible.

So it goes on. Nigel is a barrier, while Helen is open to discussion. Why is this the case when they have so much in common?

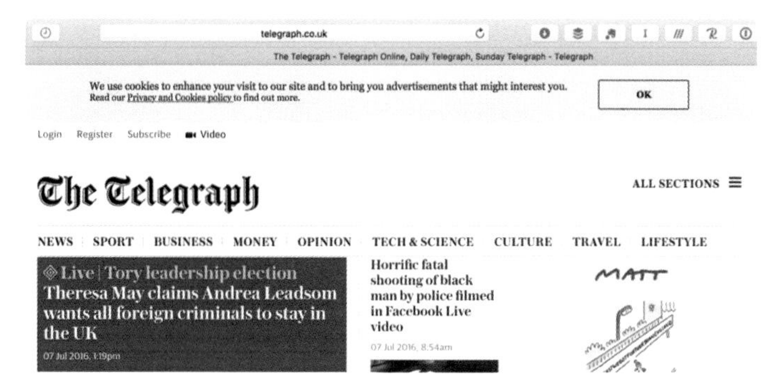

Compliance issues such as cookie notifications is just one example of how non-customer-facing staff can affect the user experience.

The answer is the amount they have to do with the customer. Nigel spends his days locked away in his office, while Helen has some friends who are customers of the business. She knows these people well, and the problems they face doing business with her company. She is also assessed on customer satisfaction as much as mitigating risk. This is not the case for Nigel.

If you think about it, most people in larger organisations have little involvement with the customer. Their jobs do not require it and they are not assessed on customer satisfaction. Instead, they focus on their own specific areas of responsibility; in the case of Nigel and Helen, mitigating risk.

When you cannot empathise with the customer you are not going to care if you damage the user experience. And if management assesses you on your ability to mitigate risk, that is going to be much higher on your agenda.

Let's look at what our group of user experience advocates can do to make colleagues think about the customer and their needs. How can they raise the profile of the customer within the organisation?

Start by helping colleagues see customers as people, rather Than Numbers In A Spreadsheet.

Humanise Your Customer

So far I have tried to keep the workload light and the enthusiasm high for your team of user experience evangelists. But now that little group needs to start doing some real work.

The primary goal is to get the attention of our colleagues and expose them to the human face of the customer. Before we go shouting about the customer, we need something to show them, something to point them at.

TELL THE CUSTOMER'S STORY

Your team of user experience evangelists will need to be able to tell the customer's story in a compelling way. They need to help colleagues empathise with customers, understand their needs and realise where they create problems for the user.

In time we will tell this story in lots of different ways, from presentations to posters. But I suggest you start by creating a small microsite that lays out the customer experience. It can include much of the information you have already pulled together in your repository; the microsite is a great place to include personas and empathy maps. Quotes and facts help to flesh out the picture colleagues will get of the customer.

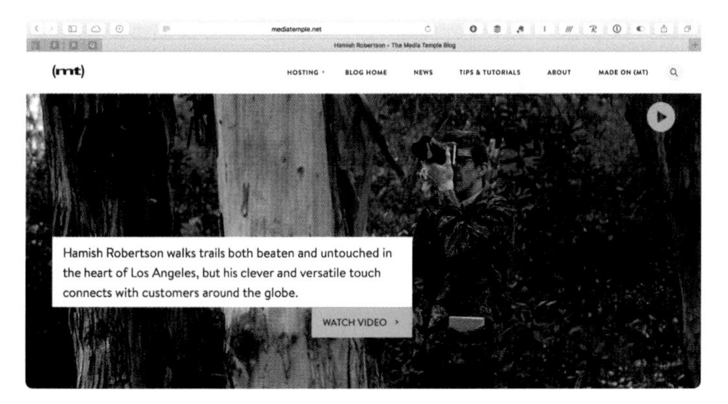

Hosting company Media Temple has made a series of videos about its customers, that help reinforce its customer focus both externally and internally.

Don't stop with the material you have. Start doing some more customer research. Creating short videos of customers can be a great way of humanising them for colleagues. Get customers talking about their lives and their experiences using your products.

I am not talking about slick, professional sales videos. Rather, you want raw, authentic video of customers talking about their experiences both good and bad. You can do this with nothing more than a smartphone and some basic editing software.

If you have already created a customer journey map this is another invaluable asset to include on the microsite. If you haven't, then later in this chapter I recommend a great opportunity to put one together.

You will need to do more than just talk about the user on your microsite. You will also need to talk about how paying attention to the customer experience benefits the organisation. You can include some of the arguments I outlined in chapter 2.

Finally, include your user experience principles. You need to show how a greater focus on customer experience would influence the way the organisation works.

One word of warning: don't just dump every piece of information you have on the microsite. Colleagues will not wade through large amounts of copy. Keep things short and concise. Where possible use infographics, photography and video rather than text. Remember that the idea is to get people thinking about the customer, not lecture them on every nuance of their behaviour. This is an internal sales tool and you need to treat it as such.

DESIGN MATTERS WHEN SELLING THE CUSTOMER

This brings me to the presentation of this microsite. It would be logical to put this content on your corporate intranet (if you have one). But although that would be the responsible thing to do, I would encourage you not to. The thing is, if your intranet is anything like most companies', nobody uses it. The user interface sucks and it is a dumping ground for every piece of documentation that exists in the company.

Create a little standalone website using something like WordPress or Squarespace. It will look so much more attractive and sell the customer much better as a result. These tools are also easy to use for those in your user experience group who are not as familiar with putting content on a website. But if they still struggle, you might have to be responsible for putting content on the microsite for them.

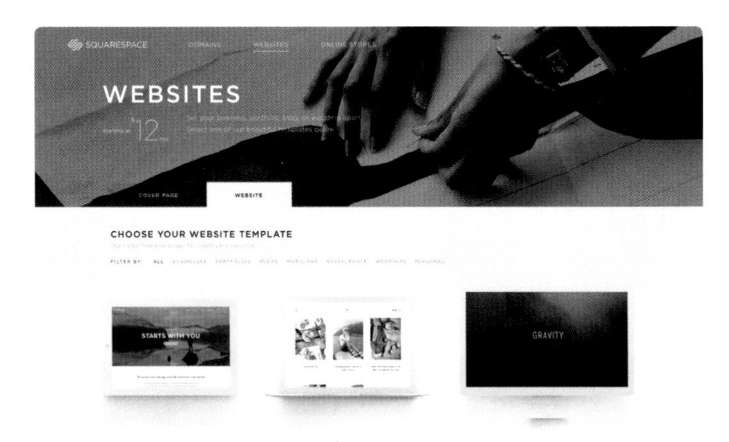

A tool like Squarespace will allow you to create an attractive microsite in a few hours. This is a much more compelling approach than putting content on your intranet.

Finally, I would recommend including a call to action on your new microsite. It is time to grow our group of user experience evangelists and this microsite will be the catalyst to do that. With that in mind I would add a newsletter sign-up form. Later in this chapter I will get into what we do with this newsletter.

Of course, having a compelling and attractive microsite is one thing. Getting people to visit it is quite another.

RUN A GUERRILLA CAMPAIGN

With our site in place it is time to tell our colleagues about it.

The obvious starting point is word of mouth. Encourage everybody in the user experience group to share it with colleagues. Get them to explain it is something they have been working on. This will make their colleagues more likely to check it out. But that alone isn't going to get you far in a larger company.

A company-wide email is another possibility – but be careful. Spamming your colleagues is not a good way to make friends. If you are going to do it, you only get one go at it, so make sure it counts. Before you send something out, make sure the microsite is as good as possible. You might want to wait until you are able to add things like customer journey maps and some data about users.

Once you feel the microsite is ready, make sure the email you send is short and apologetic. Emphasise that this is a one-off email and that it is to inform them about a resource they might find useful in their job.

Here is a sample email that you can customise to your needs.

Subject: A new resource that will help you do your job

Make sure the subject line emphasises the benefits to them. This will encourage the recipient to open the email.

Hi Paul,

If at all possible, personalise the recipient's name so it doesn't feel like a company-wide email.

Sorry to add to your already overflowing inbox. But I think I might have something you will find useful.

We all get too much email, so acknowledge you are adding to it while stating you have something they might find helpful. This will grab their attention right at the start.

I and a few others have been working on an internal resource that contains loads of information on our customers. Insights into who they are and how they behave. You can view it here.

Get to the point and provide a nice obvious link to click on.

This will be especially helpful if you don't have a huge amount of contact with customers yourself. It is always nice to know who we are trying to help at the end of the day!

It would be easy for non-customer-facing colleagues to dismiss this as not applicable to them. Take a moment to make it clear it is especially created for them and that all our roles are about helping customers.

Don't worry. This is a one-off email. I won't pester you again. But there is a danger you could miss out. We are making big strides in providing our customers with a better experience. If you want to keep up-to-date with these innovations, sign up for the newsletter on the site.

End by making it clear you won't be emailing them again and that they will miss out if they don't sign up for the newsletter. People hate feeling out of the loop so that will motivate them to take a look.

If you have any marketers in your user experience group, I am sure they can do a better job than me at writing a compelling email. The point is that you need to treat this with the same attention you would give to an external marketing campaign. You are selling user experience design, just inside the company rather than outside.

With that in mind it might also be worth sending this email using a tool like MailChimp or Campaign Monitor. This will allow you to track opens and clicks. If you work at a larger company you could even do A/B testing on your email to ensure it is as effective as possible.

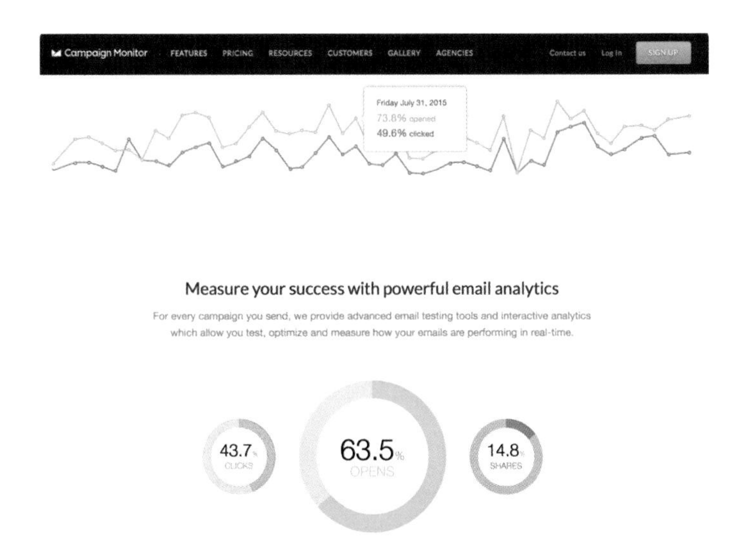

Tools like Campaign Monitor allow you to track the success of your email campaign and optimise the email you send.

Don't stop with the obvious approaches for promoting your microsite. Email and word of mouth are great but we want to keep reminding people about the customer.

Put up posters of your empathy maps or personas. Buy some mouse mats with customer quotes on them. Plaster the office with stickers including pieces from your user experience principles. Just make sure everything you do includes a call to action to the microsite.

In a perfect world you want your colleagues to be always reminded of the customer wherever they are in your office, whether in the lift or on the back of the bathroom cubical door.

I would encourage you to be a bit of a rebel and take a risk. If you ask for permission to put up posters or send out emails you can get bogged down in weeks of discussion. You can also find your crafted messages getting watered down by committees and management.

Instead, just do it – and ask for forgiveness later. Try doing things anonymously and create a bit of mystery around the whole campaign. Colleagues will wonder who is behind this guerrilla campaign. They will end up talking about it around the water cooler and that is exactly the buzz you want.

I am sure the marketers in your user experience group will have a lot more ideas than I have outlined here. But one thing I would say is that the information about your customers should be more than stories and interviews. You need to make use of data too.

Communicate With Data

Empathy and emotion are big drivers for some people. But others respond better to data. We need to ensure our internal comms campaign makes use of both stories and data. Stories make things personal. Data adds weight and authority.

Take Helen and Nigel from earlier in the chapter. Working in compliance and legal, the chances are they will be more swayed by data than stories.

Data is good for another reason: people become addicted to moving the needle. If you give people a goal they want to reach it. At the very least, they want to know how they are performing against it.

We can use data to motivate people's actions by gamifying user experience. We can even add a competitive element in some cases. To do that we need to start collecting some metrics that show the state of the user experience and make sure people are aware of them. What data should we focus on?

DATA WORTH GATHERING

One of the best things from a business perspective about this new digital world we live in is that we have a wealth of data at our fingertips. Yet this mass of data can be overwhelming. Even large organisations never get further than the default dashboard on Google Analytics.

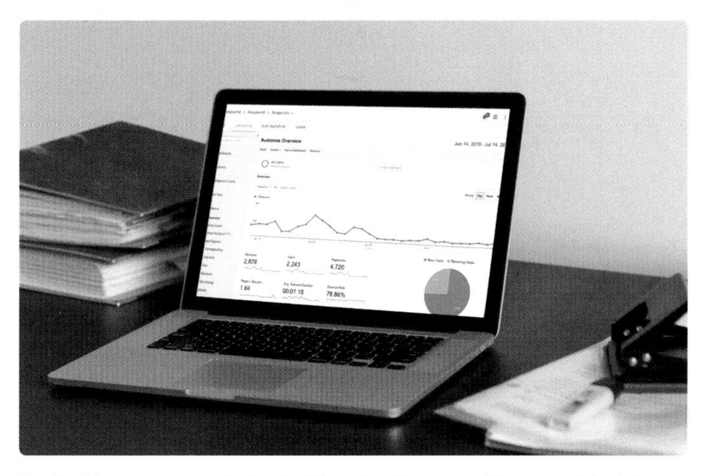

Just looking at your analytics dashboard will not provide any real insights.

But data on page reviews and user sessions aren't going to help us much from a user experience perspective. For that we will need to dig a little deeper.

That said, one metric on the default dashboard is the bounce rate. The bounce rate refers to the percentage of users who visit a page on your site only to navigate away without looking at anything else. A high bounce rate is often a sign that your site isn't meeting the needs of your users. This could be for many reasons, but it is still a figure that you can use to measure improvements in user experience.

With a bit of setup, analytics packages can offer a lot more information than a simple bounce rate percentage. Some of my favourite analytics to track include:

- **Task abandonment ratio**. The percentage of people who give up part way through a process. For example, how many people fail to complete your enquiry form or checkout process?
- **Time to complete ratio**. How long it takes for a user to complete a task. How long does it take from arriving on your website before a user signs up to your newsletter or logs in to their account?
- **Clicks to complete ratio**. How many clicks it takes for a user to complete a task. A user doesn't want to waste time clicking around a site or app trying to work out how to complete their task.
- **Error monitoring**. How many errors is your site or app generating? Errors like missing pages annoy users and damage the experience.
- **Zero search results**. How many times does a user search within your site and get no results returned? This is a sign that the site is not meeting their needs.

If that isn't enough there are other analytics packages that offer more insights into the user experience. There are apps that allow you to watch recordings of people using your site. Others show heat maps of where people click.

Among my personal favourites are tools that track rage clicks, where a user repeatedly clicks a screen element out of frustration. This is a good sign that things are not going well.

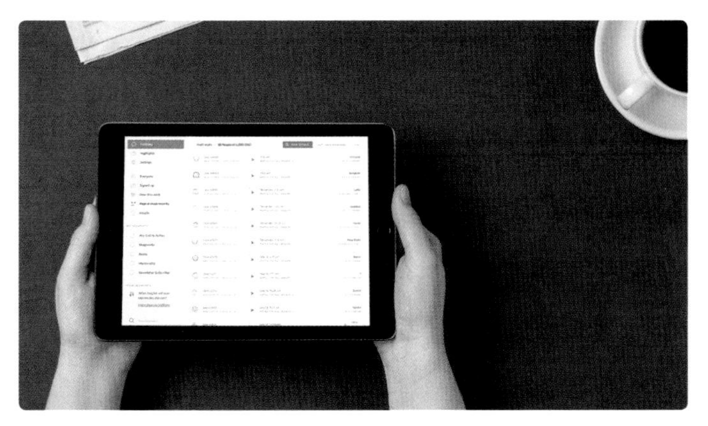

Tools like FullStory[1] provide deeper insights into the user experience.

Finally, look beyond your site analytics. Make sure you also monitor what people say about you online, especially via social media. Tools like Social Mention[2] not only track mentions, they also give you a sense of people's feelings about your brand. After all, lots of people talking about you isn't good if they are criticising your service.

You shouldn't just rely on passive analytic gathering. You should also seek out user's opinions.

1 http://smashed.by/ux33
2 http://smashed.by/ux34

ASK USERS FOR FEEDBACK

The most well-established metric for measuring customer satisfaction is the Net Promoter Score.[3] What makes the Net Promoter Score so useful is that it only requires customers to answer a single question:

How likely is it that you would recommend our company/product/service to a friend or colleague?

Answers are on a scale of 0 to 10. People who rate you with a 9 or 10 are promoters. In other words, they like your service enough to recommend it to others. Those who rate you between 0 and 6 are detractors. These people are likely to criticise you. As a result, the Net Promoter Score is a good metric to measure when monitoring user experience.

Although metrics like the Net Promoter Score and analytics can be useful indicators about the user experience, you need to be careful.

HOW TO USE YOUR DATA

Data can be a dangerous thing. For a start, it is easy to misinterpret. Take the bounce rate I mentioned earlier. A high bounce rate might not mean your website is failing. It might just mean that visitors were expecting something from

3 http://smashed.by/ux35

you that you do not provide. Incoming links or marketing material may have misled them. Of course, this is still a sign of a bad user experience, but the reason will affect how you choose to address it.

There is also a danger of focusing too much on a single metric. If all you care about is improving the Net Promoter Score, you could resort to deception to get a good score. In the short term this might work, but it will lead to longer-term consequences. That said, if you take data with a pinch of salt it can add another valuable perspective to the discussion about the customer.

You can use it to motivate people to take action. I once worked with a university where each school ran its own website. Some schools understood the value of the user experience while others did not. I struggled to get those underperforming schools on board without success. They just didn't care about the user experience.

One day in a meeting with a dean from a problematic school, I mentioned that another school was outperforming them in the ordering of prospectuses. Suddenly, his whole attitude changed. He considered his school the jewel of the university and couldn't stand the idea of another school doing better. I found him much more receptive to change from that point on.

That is why you should always seek to add metrics to the customer microsite. Also, if you can, show how one department or team is outperforming another on customer satisfaction. This can be as simple as running an ongoing survey to gather customer feedback on different parts of the process from marketing to billing. You can then show the performance on the site broken down by area of responsibility.

Adding a competitive element to customer satisfaction helps focus departments on user needs.

This will encourage a competitive element between teams, and keep people coming back to our customer microsite. That is important if we want to keep the customer in our colleagues' minds.

Ongoing Communication

Grabbing the attention of our colleagues is easy. Keeping their focus on the customer over the long term is hard. If we are going to bring about change in our organisations, we need to establish a long term communication strategy. After all, your company's culture has evolved over years. You aren't going to change that with a few emails and a microsite. This is going to take a long-term commitment.

ESTABLISH REGULAR COMMUNICATION

This is where the newsletter we discussed earlier comes in. This is going to be the backbone of our regular communications.

Our efforts should have attracted a small group of people interested in user experience design. It won't be huge to start with, and that's OK. It will grow over time if you regularly share great content in the newsletter.

This newsletter is your channel for exciting others in the company about user experience. You do this by sharing best practice, insights into your customers, and success stories. It should be a digest of lots of different content types, including but not limited to:

- Links to blog posts about user experience.
- Quotes from well-known business leaders about user experience.
- Statistics relating to user experience.
- Testimonials, tweets and reviews from your customers.
- Videos of usability sessions you have run.
- Links to new content on your customer microsite.
- Positive comments made about user experience from colleagues in the business.
- User experience success stories both within your own company and elsewhere.
- Infographics relating to user experience.

BuzzSumo[4] is an excellent tool for finding relevant content to include in your newsletter.

4 http://smashed.by/ux36

You will need a blog to support the newsletter. A place where you can post longer pieces that you cannot include in the newsletter. This blog should become a part of the customer microsite and the newsletter should link to it often. **The newsletter is the key**. A blog requires people to remember to visit it; a newsletter, you send right to their inbox.

But be careful. Don't become too precious over your blogging. Many people end up agonising over every word they write and that will kill your momentum. Publishing a blog post will become so onerous you will stop posting. Keep it short and post often.

Regularity is the key to success. If you want to change the culture in your organisation you need to make sure the customer is always in people's minds. You cannot publish a newsletter for three months and then give up because you aren't seeing widespread change. You need to be in this for the long haul.

Aim to publish on a set schedule. This will help it become a habit. People will begin to expect your newsletter in their inbox. I recommend once a fortnight. More often and you will struggle to cope with the workload; less and you won't have the impact on people's thinking. An issue of the newsletter doesn't have to be long. Aim for between three and six items. This keeps the workload down, while increasing the chances people will read it.

Don't try to do all the work yourself. Encourage members of the original user experience group to submit content. In time, you might want to invite other contributors too, as people become enthusiastic.

I would recommend using a tool like Goodbits[5] to send your newsletter. It focuses on creating a digest of useful links and content. It even has a browser extension; you can spot a great article on user experience and add it straight to the newsletter for later editing.

Goodbits makes it easy to create digest newsletters.

Be on the look out for newsletter content all the time. Don't wait until you sit down to write an issue. Follow user experience experts such as Jared Spool,[6] Gerry McGovern[7] and

5 http://smashed.by/ux37
6 http://smashed.by/ux38
7 http://smashed.by/ux39

Karen McGrane[8] on social media. Subscribe to well-known user experience blogs such as UXmatters,[9] UX Booth[10] or Smashing Magazine.[11] When something interesting pops up, add it to Goodbits ready for your next issue.

If you get stuck for content, search 'user experience' on BuzzSumo.[12] That will turn up the latest and greatest content on user experience. You can also filter by type, so if you are looking for an infographic, for example, Buzzsumo will help.

Make sure you include lots of nuggets of information on your own customers. Add the occasional success story about how you have improved the experience in your company. When you reference third-party content, write a couple of lines explaining how it applies to your company. We want to make sure the application of all this information is obvious.

Finally, send the newsletter out on a Friday lunchtime. In my experience this is when people are most looking for a distraction from their work. Of course, every company is different so experiment to find the time that gets the highest open rates.

8 http://smashed.by/ux40
9 http://smashed.by/ux41
10 http://smashed.by/ux42
11 http://smashed.by/ux43
12 http://smashed.by/ux44

Your newsletter will go a long way to raising awareness of the customer. But we want to encourage people not to just consume information about user experience design – we want them to become active.

ENCOURAGE ACTION

If people read the newsletter and then continue with business as usual we have achieved nothing. We need to encourage them to change their behaviour. But we don't need them to transform overnight. This is a marathon, not a sprint.

One small step towards action is to invite people to join our user experience evangelist group. Unlike the newsletter, this mailing list allows two-way discussion. It allows people to ask questions and start to engage with one another.
The group will continue to play a pivotal role. These are the people who believe in user experience and want to start applying the principles to their work. They will be submitting content for the newsletter. Most of all, they will be seeking ways to collaborate.

Encourage your evangelists to promote user experience in their areas of the business. Work together to create a presentation that each member of the group could share with colleagues. You may even want to start running lunchtime presentations once a quarter, a time when you invite people from across the company to attend a session on some aspect of user experience design. I have spoken at many such events and they are popular. Laying on some food always helps attendance!

If you can secure some budget, getting the occasional outside speaker makes all the difference. An outside speaker creates more buzz and they tend to have a greater perceived authority.

Of course, sessions like this don't put colleagues in front of real users, and that has to be the ultimate aim. I have sat in on many usability sessions where people were watching a session for the first time. Without fail, they have a lightbulb moment where they realise the importance of user experience.

With that in mind why not open our usability test sessions to anybody who wants to attend. You are running usability test sessions, aren't you?

Make them a regular event. For example, hold usability testing on the third Friday morning of each month. Test whatever you are currently working on with three users and invite your colleagues to attend. Then sit down over lunch and discuss what you saw.

If you promote this enough through the newsletter, people will come to expect it and a few people will start turning up.

Word will spread and given time it will become an established part of the company calendar.

Given time, commitment and patience you will begin to move user experience to the front of people's minds. It won't happen overnight. It will start slow and grow at what feels like a painful pace. Things will pick up speed as word spreads. A point may come where you feel the organisation needs an injection of energy to move to the next level. You might want to go for a big splash.

Make A Big Splash

Dear Paul,
We are running a leadership conference on creating an outstanding customer experience. We wondered whether you would consider being a speaker. The conference is taking place in Hong Kong...

It was at this point I stopped reading. I had always wanted to go to Hong Kong and I was like an overexcited child. I had also worked with these people before, so I knew it would be a fun event. They were a large Asian insurance company and they knew how to do things in style!

Sure enough, it was an impressive event. The conference took place in the Ritz Carlton, the highest hotel in the world. The party on the second night of the conference was incredible: food from across the region, magicians, dancers and a gorgeous setting. Alcohol flowed and everybody had a great time.

Holding an internal conference in the highest hotel on the planet is one way to make a splash!

The speakers were amazing too. I am a confident speaker, but the calibre was so high I felt quite intimidated! By the end of the two days, the audience of 120 leaders went away inspired and equipped to improve the experience of their customers.

The executive of that insurance company knew that sometimes it takes a big splash to grab attention, and that by doing so they could focus staff on what matters.

You might not have the budget for such a lavish affair.

No doubt you feel daunted at putting on a company-wide event. But don't dismiss an internal conference out of hand. I am not suggesting you do it on day one. Build up to it. Run a few lunchtime events first. It is worth the effort if you can find the time and budget.

An internal conference is a chance to enthuse people, get them thinking and engage them in change. But what would an event like that look like?

SESSIONS TO INCLUDE IN A BIG SPLASH EVENT

Over the years I have spoken at hundreds of events both internal and external. In that time I've come to learn what works and what does not. It turns out that the key is to have different types of sessions.

I have been to some events that have just included a lineup of external speakers. Unfortunately, the speakers lack the inside knowledge of the organisation. They couldn't talk about how user experience applies to day-to-day operations.

I also know of other events which have relied on internal speakers. These events have lacked the inspiration that comes from looking outside the organisation. The best events are those that include a mix: external experts who bring inspiration and a new perspective; internal speakers who can provide more practical insights.

The best events include a mix of external and internal speakers.

The last thing people want is to spend the whole day listening to lectures on how they should care more about the needs of users. A good event should have an interactive component to it as well.

There are lots of opportunities to run breakout groups and small workshops, chances to investigate different parts of user experience design best practice. These breakout groups are a great time to develop personas, empathy maps and customer journey maps. They are also a great opportunity for things like:

- Learning about usability testing.
- Discussing how to overcome barriers to change.
- Sessions on prioritising user groups.

These sessions provide a chance for people to express their opinions. This makes them feel listened to, which is vital if you wish to get people on your side. It is also important to get people thinking about user needs rather than just listening to a lecture.

Of course, talking about the benefits of sessions such as these is easy. The logistics of putting together an event like this may feel intimidating.

LOGISTICS TO CONSIDER

Let me be honest with you. Although a big splash event is a great way to stimulate an interest in user experience design, it is a lot of work to organise.

For a start you will need to find a venue capable of holding your entire audience while at the same time allowing breakout groups. This will be hard because you will not know exactly how many people will attend. I recommend asking for RSVPs before booking the final venue so that you have an idea of numbers – but expect a reasonable number of dropouts at the last minute.

Book a venue that is too small for the number of people you expect to attend. This will accommodate last minute drop-outs, and will ensure that the event feels busy. Nothing is worse than a few people rattling around in a massive room.

It is tempting to schedule the event to ensure key individuals are able to attend. I would suggest you do not take this approach. In my experience it is difficult to achieve. But I've also discovered that people are more likely to attend if they fear missing out.

When planning the event, consider catering. If at all possible make sure the catering is high quality. Some good food makes a huge difference to how people perceive the event.

Finally, think about how you intend to promote the event. It is important that you create a real buzz around it. That is going to involve more work than just sending out an email invitation.

Which brings us to the elephant in the room.

FINDING THE TIME

You will have noticed that the amount of work I'm asking from you has increased the further into the book you have read. To begin with, I asked you to assemble a few people who shared your passion for user experience design.

Now we find ourselves considering running an internal event designed to make a big splash. This will involve a lot of work.

The trouble is, few companies give staff the space in their schedules to do this kind of strategic work. Instead, we spend our days with business as usual and crisis management. How, then, are you going to find time to build a user experience culture?

I do not claim it will be easy. Neither do I claim to have all the answers. After all, I do not know the specifics of your role. I would encourage you to take a step back and redefine how you perceive your role.

We have a tendency to define our role around deliverables. We code websites, create design comps, write copy or produce campaigns. But if we are to forge a user experience design culture within our organisations we need to redefine our role.

We need to become educators as much as we are implementers. Our job is no longer just to produce deliverables but to become change makers. It is our job to promote the needs of users within our organisation. At times, this part of our job may need to take priority over the deliverables we produce.

We will have to make some hard decisions about how we spend our time. We will need to get better at saying no. Some things we used to do will have to take a back-seat to this new work. Most of us have a considerable amount of autonomy over what we do and when we do it. That said, I am aware that sooner or later we will need managerial support.

Get Managerial Support

Andrew was one of the nicest people I've ever had the privilege of working with. He had been working as a full-stack web developer within an internal digital team of a charity for the last eleven years. Before that he had been a Church of England minister. He still had that soft-spoken demeanour one expects from an English vicar.

A caring and gentle person, you never heard him say a harsh word about his colleagues. Most of the time he was positive; and yet right now his round face was screwed up in a look of resignation.

"You are right. We need to start with user needs," he began. "But getting the executive to think like that just isn't going to happen."

It turns out Andrew had tried many times to get management to think about user experience without success. He had concluded it just wasn't going to be possible and to be honest I didn't blame him. As I listened to Andrew talk about his attempts, Jared Spool's article flitted through my mind – the one about not being able to convince the executive of anything.

But things were different this time. We had been working hard to raise the profile of user experience among colleagues. Our newsletter and blog posts had attracted a lot of interest and there was a general buzz around the idea of customer experience.

There was more that we wanted to do. But we knew that to do those things we needed management's support. The time will come when you will have done all you can behind the scenes. You will need permission to take the next big step.

Where that line is and what that next big step will be will vary from company to company. It might be to run an internal conference. Or it could be to carry out a pilot project (something we will get to in the next chapter).

What I would say is do as much as you can before going to management. The longer you leave it, the more momentum will be behind your cause and the more compelling your case will be. You will have more support, more statistics, more stories. In short, you will be better prepared. That will be important if you want management to take you seriously.

Get The Attention Of Management

Whether the executive of a large multinational, or your line manager, getting their attention can be tough. It is going to take patience and perseverance.

You will find yourself going through the same process with each layer of management in what can feel like an endless cycle. But remember, your job is as much an educator as an implementer. Nobody said building a user experience culture was going to be easy.

It would be tempting to go to management asking permission for whatever it is you want to do next. For example, you might want to run a big splash event. But that is not going to get their attention. At least, not in a positive way.

Management get requests like this all the time, from people who want permission, time and funding for some project or initiative. They spend their lives knocking back half-baked ideas and rejecting good ideas they don't have the budget for.

If we want to get their attention, we need to be different. That is why we are going to start by going to them with nothing but good news. After all, that almost never happens! A member of staff, proactively going out of their way to make a positive difference to the business. Who has ever heard of that?

But before we can do that, we need to find out what they care about.

APPLY UX DESIGN PRINCIPLES TO MANAGEMENT NEEDS

If you want to get management's attention you need to know what they care about. This will allow you to frame your pitch around that interest. As Jared Spool said in his post.

You can find out what your executives are already convinced of. If they are any good at what they do, they likely have something they want to improve. It's likely to be related to improving revenues, reducing costs, increasing the number of new customers, increasing the sales from existing customers, or increasing shareholder value.

Good UX can help with each of those things."

Take a moment to think about your immediate line manager. What does that person care about? Maybe it's meeting an annual target. Maybe it's achieving the budgetary cuts imposed on them. If you want to be cynical, maybe it's getting their annual bonus.

Once you know that, you can frame the work you have been doing with user experience within that context. It may take a little imagination, but it is possible.

Let's imagine your manager is the head of marketing. She has had her budget cut for the third year in a row and she's looking for cost savings. Going to her and asking her to spend money on a big pilot project is a waste of time. Instead, you need to start by helping with her immediate problem.

Make some small incremental improvements to the website, changes that encourage more social shares and maybe boost your Net Promoter Score. Talk to some users and get testimonial saying they were more likely to recommend the brand because of the good experience.

Once you have made some positive changes, now is the time to go to your manager. Don't go to her with problems and requests. Go to her with positive feedback. Tell her about the tweaks you have made. Tell her about the fact users seem more willing to promote the brand after improvements to user experience. Say that if you can continue to make these kinds of improvements it might increase word-of-mouth recommendation. This should, in time, decrease expenditure on advertising.

This is the kind of conversation that makes management's day. You have shown an understanding of the problems the department faces and taken steps to address it. If you can go back to her with good news like that two or three times you will find her much more receptive when you ask her for something.

FRAME YOUR REQUEST AROUND MANAGEMENT'S AGENDA

After you have established some credibility with your manager it is much easier to go to her with requests. But even so, it is still important you frame those requests in the right way. You still have to prove that the request is going to benefit your manager or at least the department.

If you want to run a big splash event your manager will want to know what benefits it will provide. Not benefits to the user and, to be honest, not even benefits to the company as a whole: she will want to know the benefits to her and her department. In other words, you are applying user-centric thinking to your own management. You are identifying their needs and addressing them.

Talk about how an event like that would raise the profile of the marketing function, or that if we could get cross-departmental support it might help raise funding for a user experience project – a project that would increase brand perception.

Whatever it is you're asking for, frame it in the context of management's agenda. Maybe your manager wants to increase revenue. Make sure you can show your request will help address that; if you cannot, you might have to change your request.

Most of all you will have to put the work in to prove that your idea is worth spending time on. That means spending as much time as possible up front working out how best to present it.

Show, Don't Tell

How would you convince the executive team of Disney to invest $1 billion to renovate their entire Disneyland resorts to improve the user experience? That was the challenge facing one small team within Disney who had an idea.

They wanted staff to greet visitors to the Disneyland park by name. They wanted Mickey and the other Disney characters to be able to seek out and wish children a happy birthday. They wanted adults to never have to worry about paying for things or losing their hotel keys. In short they wanted to make the Disney experience even more magical.

They aimed to achieve this by giving every visitor a wrist-band with an RFID chip in it. This would identify them and their location in the park. This simple band would offer up a wealth of possibilities.

The Disney MagicBand involved a significant investment for the Disney executive team.

By associating their credit card details with a band, people could pay for anything in the park. The greeters at restaurants could see people approaching and greet them by name.

There would be administrative benefits too. Disney could see where people were in the park and so could control the flow of visitors and staffing.

There was so much potential. But tapping into this potential was a huge investment in renovations. Something as simple as allowing the band to open a hotel door would mean replacing every lock.

The team could have chosen to go to the executive with a business plan. But that wouldn't have done the idea justice. This is an important lesson to learn. To understand an experience, people need to experience it. A document is not going to get the job done for two reasons.

First, a document will not sell the experience. User experience is hard to quantify. To get buy in from the executive they needed to experience it. They needed to see and feel what the user would see and feel. Second, a document has limited capability to create a shared understanding. Different people will interpret what that experience will be like in different ways. The nuances of the experience get lost, and when it comes to creating a great experience the devil is in the detail.

So how did the team at Disney convince their management to invest $1 billion? They showed them what the experience would be like, rather than telling them.

They took an unused warehouse on a backlot of Disney and built a prototype.[1] Using nothing more than some plywood and cardboard, they built a low fidelity mock-up of key locations in the park.

1 http://smashed.by/ux45

When the team finished, they invited the executives to come and view it. Each executive got a dummy wristband and were guided around the warehouse. They were asked to touch the wristband to the hotel door and somebody behind the scenes would 'beep' and open the door. They were greeted by name as they walked up to the mock-up's restaurant. And so it went on. Each stage of the experience was made real to help the executive feel what it would be like for users.

This principle of show, don't tell is the cornerstone of selling user experience. If you want management to invest, you need to give them a taste of what they will be getting. If you want to throw a big splash event, hold a smaller event first and get at least one of them along. If you want to run a pilot project, produce a basic mock-up first, something to give them a sense of what they will get.

This approach will get them excited about the direction you want to go. It will help them feel the experience. But by itself this won't be enough. You will need to validate your approach too.

Validate Your Arguments

You are not going to convince a finance director to spend money based on school room art projects. Far more executives make decisions based on gut instinct than would care to admit. But appealing to them on that basis alone will not be enough. We need something more tangible.
There are four approaches available to us to add credibility to our case for investment. These are:

- Data validation.
- User validation.
- External expert validation.
- Comparable case studies.

The most compelling of these is data.

COLLECT DATA

If you can associate specific figures with your request, you will find management much more likely to accept it.

Let's imagine you want to introduce live chat to your website, so users can get support as they navigate. You would start by establishing how many simultaneous chat conversations an operator can handle. Next, take the number of calls you receive and the cost per call. You can then calculate the cost savings live chat would provide.

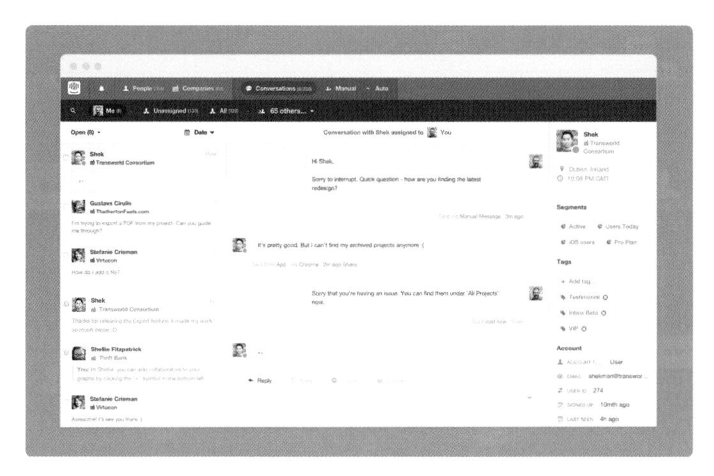

Live chat systems like Intercom are much more cost-effective than call centres. This makes showing the return on an investment in user experience easy.

Another example could be improvements to a checkout. If you want to improve a checkout, it is straightforward to make predictions about the increase in revenue.

But not all improvements to the user experience are so easy to quantify. Then there are managers who have already decided they don't want to invest in your idea – data will not convince them. All this means you cannot rely on data alone. Which brings us on to user feedback.

GATHER USER FEEDBACK

User feedback is a way for management to see the reality of the user experience. People in management often have little contact with users, finding themselves detached from the experience. You need to bridge that gap. As I said earlier, you need to humanise the user.

We have already discussed ways of doing this with your colleagues. The same principles apply with management. Showing videos of users struggling with the existing experience is particularly powerful. Even better is getting management to sit in on a usability test session.

The great thing about exposing management to users is that they can draw their own conclusions. They don't have to rely on your interpretation. The sad truth is that they don't respect your opinion as much as they should. That is why an external perspective can also be helpful.

GET AN EXTERNAL PERSPECTIVE

I want to let you in on a secret. One of the first things I do when I am asked to consult for a company is sit down with the internal team and ask them what needs to be done. Almost without fail they know what needs to happen. Here is the embarrassing bit: much of the time I just repeat that to management. Why doesn't management just listen to its own staff, rather than hiring me? There are two reasons.

First, internal teams often lack the communication skills to convince management. A big part of my job is to sell management on ideas. Presentation is everything, as I am sure you have gathered by this point in the book.

Second, management often feels the need for an external, unbiased perspective. They have employees coming to them all the time with an agenda. An external consultant doesn't carry that kind of baggage. So there are times when getting an outside perspective might help to sell an idea.

But that doesn't always have to involve hiring a consultant like me. Quoting books like this one or referring management to online posts and reports can sometimes be enough. A similar option is to refer to what other companies have been doing.

FIND COMPARABLE CASE STUDIES

Most management teams are risk-averse. This means we need to reduce the size of the risk in their minds. One way to do this is to refer to others who have taken a similar approach.

The more similarities, the more compelling the case. Ideally, you want a direct competitor who has done exactly the same thing and made it work. I say ideally. In fact, it's not an ideal circumstance at all, because it means your company is playing catch-up. But an example like that will motivate management.

Failing that, look for examples of big names. If IBM or General Electric does something then most management teams will consider it a good idea. In truth, it might not be, but that is how management tends to think in my experience.

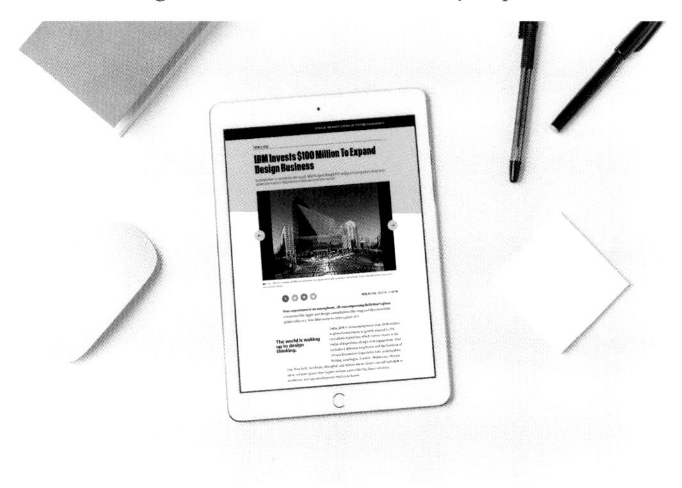

When a big name like IBM invests in user experience, others are likely to follow suit.

What you will find is that if you can combine some real-life examples with your data and a working prototype, management will listen. Now we need to get their approval.

Get Management's Approval

I sat back feeling rather smug. That was one hell of a presentation, even if I did say so myself. I had just finished presenting to a charity's management team. I had shown how they should invest in user experience, rather than pouring money into advertising as they had done in the past. I had proved this would significantly improve donations.

The presentation had everything: some mock-ups to help them understand what the improvements would look like; data on how those improvements would translate into donations; videos of users interacting with the old and new versions. The whole thing was watertight.

I laid out their next steps. They needed to put on hold their advertising campaign for the next year and redesign their website from the ground up. It was a big job, but my presentation won them over. There were details to work out, but I secured their agreement.

I went away confident that I would get the approval the internal team needed to move forward. Yet a month later, nothing had happened. What had gone wrong?

I agonised over this question for years. As I got more experienced with other companies I eventually realised my mistake. I had overwhelmed them. The size of the challenge had frightened them and they reacted by burying their head in the sand. It happens a lot and can destroy momentum for change.

Since then, I have got better in these situations. When I present to management today it consists of three steps:

- Scare them.
- Inspire them.
- Start small.

SCARE YOUR MANAGEMENT

Right back in chapter 1, I talked about the need to scare management into action. Nothing motivates people like the threat of something taken away. If you can prove that the status quo is under threat they will react.

The problem with scaring people is you can overwhelm them. You have to offer a solution. You cannot just present them with the threat. If you do, they will feel overwhelmed and try to ignore it. You have to offer them some form of salvation.

INSPIRE MANAGEMENT

Once you have established the danger, you must provide a solution. But you cannot stop there. You must also excite them about the future. That is what the Disney MagicBand demonstration did – it inspired management about what was possible.

For you it might be a small prototype before a bigger pilot project. It might be a series of small workshops before a big splash event. The point is to give management a glimpse of the future, at what could be.

But even that can overwhelm them.

GIVE MANAGEMENT A SIMPLE NEXT STEP

If you imagined standing on the top of Mount Everest seeing the world stretching out below you, chances are you would feel inspired. But if you are anything like me, the journey to get there is insurmountable. No pun intended.

The view from a mountaintop is inspiring. But the journey to get there can be daunting.

The harder the journey, the more resistance you will meet from management. Ask them to approve a project that is going to cost a lot of money or take a lot of time and you will struggle. Ask them to take a small step towards that bigger project and they are much more likely to say yes.

This is not just because you remove the sense of being overwhelmed. It is also because you are reducing the perceived risk. Their decision isn't going to cost a lot of money if it goes wrong. It is only going to cost the next step.

A great example of this is the pilot project. A pilot project is a small step that allows management to validate an idea. It doesn't feel like a big request and so is more likely to get approved, especially when it addresses an area of concern to management. It is this idea of a pilot that we are going to address in the next chapter.

Develop A Proof Of Concept

Whether it is convincing management or your colleagues, by now it must be apparent that the way to do this is by showing them success. We need to show them the benefits of user experience design. This raises an interesting question: if creating a great user experience is so beneficial, why don't you already have success stories?

I am presuming you have been concerned about the user's experience for a while. I am also presuming you have a good understanding of what is involved in creating a good user experience. Why, then, don't you have lots of compelling examples of success?

Part of the problem may have been convincing management to allow you to focus on the user experience. As we established in the previous chapter, that can be a challenge. But I suspect that is not the only problem.

In most cases, the real barriers to implementing the principles of user experience design are external constraints: constraints of the technology; constraints around compliance and policies; constraints around requirements. These limitations have prevented you from ever showing what a great user experience looks like.

As we know, if we want to get colleagues and management on board we need to inspire them. Sooner or later we have to be able to show them what good looks like.

We can do this in lots of ways. We can show them examples from other companies. We can prototype small experiences through wireframing, or incremental improvements to existing touchpoints. But there are limits as to how compelling these will be. Eventually, you'll need to really show what user experience design can do. At that point, you will need a proof of concept, a pilot project that can act as an example of how user experience design can transform your company for the better.

An Experiment In User Experience Design

It is important that you position this pilot project in the right way. You need to position it as an experiment, as a research and development project, if you will. Do not suggest this will be more widely implemented. In fact, play down its importance as much as possible.

This may seem counter-intuitive. After all, you are looking to promote user experience design. Why would you downplay the showcase for user experience design best practice? Because we want your pilot to be free from constraints.

The higher the profile of your pilot project, the more attention it will receive; the more attention, the more your colleagues will want their say; the more people interfere, the more constraints will be placed on the project.

Instead, your pilot project should be positioned as an imagining of what the user experience could be. It shouldn't focus on integrating with back-end technology. It should be unconcerned with practicalities or other limitations. It is a chance to dream dreams and experiment.

By positioning the project as an experiment, it becomes less threatening to colleagues. An experiment is disposable. An experiment isn't a serious proposition. It can get away with slaughtering some sacred cows.

I am not saying it won't receive any pushback. If you start proposing changes that impinge on other departments you can expect comments from them. But you can use the project's experimental status as a chance to defuse arguments.

You might be wondering what the point of a pilot project is if it's downplayed so much. Simple: people want what they can see. If you can create an exciting, inspiring pilot, people will want it. That shifts the burden of proof.

It falls to you to prove the benefits of user experience and that those benefits are worth everybody else changing. You have to explain why legacy technology should be replaced, why policies should be changed, why departments need to work differently. That is a big job. You have to fight every one of those battles.

If you can create a proof of concept that key stakeholders get excited about, it shifts that dynamic. People will start to ask why IT can't implement it. They'll want to know what is stopping the policy changes. Instead of people asking why, they are starting to ask, why not.

Of course, that makes picking the right pilot project an important decision.

Pick The Right Pilot

With so much riding on a successful pilot project, you might find deciding what to focus on to be a big challenge. It doesn't have to be. There is no reason why you have to do a single pilot project. There are good arguments for running a series of them.

First, a truly inspiring pilot project will not be built overnight. It takes time, money and people to get it off the ground – getting management to sign off on that is not going to be easy. Instead of going for that kind of project out of the gate, it makes sense to start with something smaller. Second, a smaller pilot is going to cause less fuss. It is going to tread on fewer toes and attract less attention. But it will prove to management that pilots are worthwhile and sets a precedent for this way of working. If you run a few smaller pilot projects, when you work on something larger it will be easier to get approval and also ruffle fewer feathers among colleagues.

So what makes a good pilot project?

Look for something small and self-contained that can be prototyped in a week or so of work, something it is easy to define the edges of. Most of all, go for something that management care about.

I once worked on a pilot project focused on approving expenses, simply because I knew a key stakeholder hated the application he had to use and the hoops he had to jump through. My ultimate aim was to redesign the company intranet. But I knew if I could show this stakeholder the benefits of a well-designed interface, it would make it easier to get him to back an intranet redesign.

Now that might be an extreme example. But what it shows is that a pilot project is more about getting internal buy-in than transforming the user experience on day one.

Once you have proved the value of a small pilot, go for something with a bit more profile: maybe a redesign of your website's homepage, or something that will involve a few more stakeholders but that is relatively self-contained and can be done quickly. This will give you a chance to prove the worth of pilots and also improve your ability to deliver quickly.

Delivering A Successful Pilot Project

How you go about delivering your pilot is almost as important as the result itself. I know you know how to build great user experiences, but this isn't just about the user experience. It is about introducing your organisation to a different mindset. We need the right people involved and we need to work in the right way. It also means making the most of the final result.

PUT TOGETHER THE RIGHT TEAM

It would be tempting to assemble a team of user experience professionals to work on your pilot: designers, developers, copywriters. You would deliver a great user experience, but you wouldn't do much to build a user experience culture. After all, these people already understand user experience. Instead, we need a mixed team.

Getting the balance right is important. You need people in the group who grasp user experience so the team has the right culture, but you also need the others too: stakeholders who have an interest in the project but need educating.

By including other stakeholders in the team you get to expose them to this new way of thinking. With any luck they will become converts and take that thinking back to their own team. They will start promoting user-centric thinking beyond the project. The culture of our pilot project will start to infect the rest of the organisation like a virus.

But more than that, they will be advocates for the pilot. Because they helped create it they will feel ownership of it and they will defend it to colleagues.

For that to work, we need to establish a new culture and that means working in the right way. To achieve this I recommend three rules of piloting.

THE THREE RULES OF PILOTING

In the next chapter we will talk more about practical tips for building around user needs. Also, for smaller pilot projects I recommend design sprints, an approach created by the Google Ventures team. But for now I want to focus on three rules for running pilot projects, rules that will ensure the project has the right focus.

The most important rule to establish for your pilot projects is that the only constraint is the user need. You are not designing for the business. You are not working within organisational constraints. You are delivering the best experience possible for the user.

Don't misunderstand me. I am not suggesting business objectives are unimportant. I am just saying that in the context of a pilot, they are secondary to user needs. The aim is to create a great user experience first. We need to focus stakeholders on that and not let them get distracted by organisational thinking.

Establish this up front and remind those involved of this fact – often. If you don't, you will find that people will constrain their thinking.

The second rule is to always test. Test your pilot often with real users. If you disagree over the best approach, test. If you have suggested a solution, test. If you have revised a previously tested solution, test again.

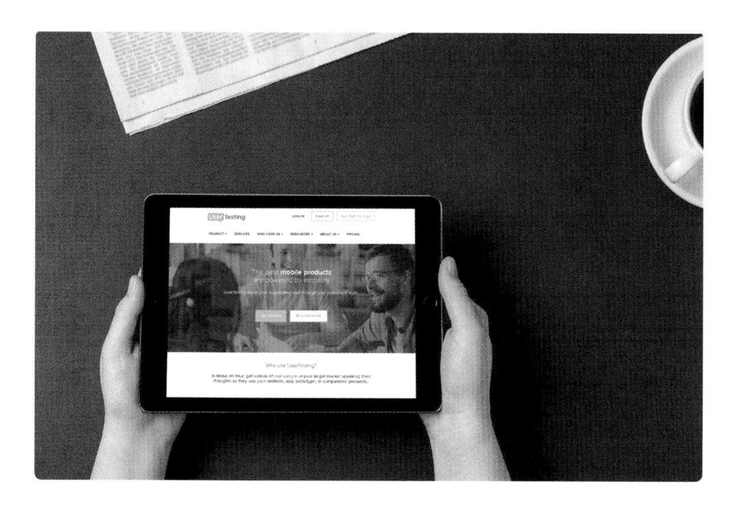

Usabilty testing can be quick and dirty. Try services like UserTesting.[1]

Quick and dirty testing is fine. Use services like UserTesting[2] or grab family members. You don't need real customers, just anybody outside of the organisation.

My third rule is that a pilot team should always work together in a room. I will go further into the importance of collaboration in the next chapter. For now I just want to emphasise how important it is that all team members sit and work together every day. It is the only way you will establish the right culture.

1 http://smashed.by/ux46
2 http://smashed.by/ux47

I have a fourth rule for piloting. Running a pilot should be an open and transparent process. But that brings me to promoting the pilot.

PROMOTE YOUR PILOT

Running a pilot carries with it two dangers. First, that like a customer journey map, your pilot project disappears into a drawer never to see the light of day again. Second, that colleagues see the pilot project as a secret, stealth project and feel excluded from contributing.

This second issue is particularly important in some organisations. If people hear about the pilot project on the grapevine, they will feel that you have excluded them and this will lead them to become resentful. That is a good reason for being open and transparent about what you are doing.

Although I talked about downplaying the importance of the pilot, I was not suggesting you should do it in secret. In fact, the opposite is true.

Make use of your newsletter, blog and the other channels you have established to explain why you are doing the project and its role in the organisation. This is your chance to explain it is an experiment and isn't a threat.

But don't stop there. While the pilot is happening you need to invest time in sharing what it is you are doing and why. Be open and transparent about the way you are working and the decisions you are making. Talk about what is working and what is not.

When the project finishes, make sure it is available for all to see and try out. Publish an explanation of the final result. I find that a video colleagues have to watch before seeing the pilot is often a good way of ensuring your message gets across.

A video overlay which explains your prototype will manage expectations and improve the quality of feedback.

Finally, make sure you share the lessons learned and provide a way people can share their feedback.

All this will help people feel consulted and it will also help introduce them to a user-centric way of working. Most of all, this is your opportunity to excite them about the possibilities.

Unfortunately, all this will take time.

Find The Time For Your Pilot

Time is one of the biggest barriers to running pilot projects. Most organisations don't leave a lot of time for employees to work on strategic projects. They try to maximise efficiencies. Most employees are working at full capacity with business as usual.

You are going to need to carve out time for any pilot projects and that means you will need permission. But it is not enough to go to management and ask for that time. Even if you present a compelling case, your manager will want to know how you are going to deal with the other work you have on your plate. I won't claim finding time will be easy, but you can start to solve this problem with the three Ds:

- Discard
- Delegate
- Defer

If you sit down and look at what you do every day, you maybe shocked how much of it you can discard. Many of the things we end up doing in our job made sense once upon a time, but things change.

Many of us know that some of what we do adds little value to the business – we simply haven't stopped because we didn't have the justification. Now you do. Now you have something more worthwhile to replace it with. The interest you have been building in user experience will justify replacing those pointless tasks.

Unfortunately we cannot discard all the tasks we do, but we can delegate some of them. Others could do much of the work I see internal digital teams doing if they received a little bit of training. Updating the website, adding news stories, managing social media channels.

It would be possible to delegate these, at least for a period of time, to colleagues. Where that isn't possible you could hire a temp to do business-as-usual work. This would allow you to focus on the more strategic pilot projects.

Finally, look for work that you could defer. Everybody likes to think their projects are urgent, but that is rarely the case. Don't just accept your colleagues deadlines: push back. A pilot project shouldn't be a second-class citizen simply because it doesn't have an arbitrary deadline.

By using the three Ds you should be able to lighten your load enough for a small pilot project. Once that project proves its value, it will strengthen the case for discarding, delegating or deferring more.

One word of warning: resist the temptation to assign part of your time to a pilot project. You need to block out a chance to work on a pilot full-time. If you are part-time it will always be the thing that gets squeezed out. It will also make coordinating with colleagues harder. If you have a team of people, assign some to provide support and others to work on the pilot. Although it is tempting, do not give everybody a chance to work on the pilot part-time. Admittedly, those stuck on support won't be happy, but they will get to work on the next pilot. Splitting people's time rarely works.

The only exception to this rule will be other stakeholders from across the organisation. Persuading colleagues to give up a week of their time to work full-time on a pilot would be hard. Getting them to commit to even longer will be impossible.

Instead, get them in the room full-time. Suggest that they work alongside the rest of the team even if they are working on other things at the same time as the pilot. This will allow you to engage them in the pilot, while still letting them deal with business as usual.

In my experience they often get drawn deeper into the project if they are sitting in the room with the rest of the team.

I know finding time will be hard. You might not be able to do everything I have suggested above. That is OK. If you cannot get stakeholders in the room, that is fine. If you have to work on a pilot part-time, that is better than nothing. But don't settle for that without trying. At least try to block out your time. Push hard to get stakeholders in the room. Sometimes we think things are going to be impossible and don't try, yet often things turn out to be easier than we expected.

Running a successful pilot project will take some trial and error. Having the right mix of people in the room will make a huge difference. When you get it right your pilot projects will become an exemplar for a new mindset within the organisation, a new way of working that focuses on the needs of users. It is this new way of working that we look at in the next chapter.

Establish Better Working Practices

Do you ever experience imposter syndrome? That feeling that you will be exposed as a fraud? That you are not the expert others perceive you to be? I do, which is probably not what you want to hear from the author of a book you are reading. You want me to be the expert with all the answers. But much of the time I don't feel like that.

Never have I felt like an imposter more acutely than when working with Hannah and her team. Hannah was the head of a world-class digital team in a high-profile organisation. She had a great reputation and I had followed her work for some time.

Hannah and her team knew their stuff. They knew how to build amazing user experiences. Yet they had invited me to work with them. Why? What did they think I could tell them that they didn't already know?

It turned out that although they were experts in their field, they were constantly prevented from doing their best work by the organisational culture. They found themselves compromising their work just to get it out of the door in a difficult environment.

Chances are, you are in the same position. You know how to create great experiences – this book isn't about teaching you that. What it is about is helping you seize the opportunity to use what you know. It is about building a culture that allows you to use best practice in user experience design. In this chapter we focus on the practicalities of building around the user's experience. How do we get to build digital services the right way?

Real life is about compromise. It is about knowing which battles to fight. But what should you compromise over and when should you stick to your principles?

When it comes to building a user experience culture, the reality is that individual decisions are less important than the way you work. It is worth compromising over the small things to win the war. It is often worth giving in over little usability issues such as marketing wanting unnecessary form fields. Yes, these damage the user experience, but it is better to keep your colleagues on board.

What matters is that you do not compromise over how you work: your methodology. If you get the methodology right, it will encourage the right thinking in your colleagues. If you can do that, the smaller battles will eventually decrease.

What are those ways of working that shouldn't be compromised? Well, kicking off a project in the right way should definitely be at the top of the list.

Begin With User Needs

How do most of your projects begin? If you're like my clients, they begin with a colleague from another department coming to you with a need they have. Maybe they need a micro-site to support a marketing campaign. Maybe they need somewhere to post job advertisements online. Maybe they need a mobile app because your competition has one.

There is nothing wrong with this starting point. But it isn't going to help build a user experience culture. Such an approach is inward-looking. It focuses on the needs of individual departments, or at best the business as a whole. From the outset, you frame the project within the context of what the organisation wants to achieve. This may or may not be in line with what the user wants to do. If it is not, then you are going to face an uphill battle to make the project a success. Instead, you should begin with the user's needs.

HOW TO BEGIN WITH THE USER'S NEEDS

When a colleague comes to you with an idea for a project, always start by reframing the project around user needs. I mean immediately. Before you do anything else. This set of user needs becomes the brief for the project.

Step one in this process is to get the internal client to identify which part of the customer journey you are hoping to help with. This is where the customer journey map will help.

Sit down with the client and ask them to show you on the customer journey map where they feel the project fits in. If they cannot, discuss with them what they feel is missing from the customer journey map.

Notice the approach I took there. I didn't challenge the validity of the project. I worked from the assumption the customer journey map wasn't representative. This helps in two ways. First, it prevents your internal client from becoming defensive, because you are not attacking their idea. Second, it keeps the conversation focused on the user need.

These conversations sometimes lead to improvements in the customer journey map. But more often they lead to the client's idea becoming more customer-centric.

Once you have done that, define what the project is going to deliver – but not around functionality. Instead, define what user needs it will fulfil.

A great way of doing that is a user story card. A user story card consists of three simple statements.

- I am...
- I want to...
- So I can...

A typical user story card for the Apple website might be:

I am a designer at an ad agency. I want to buy an iPad Pro and Pencil, so I can use them for illustration work.

User story cards provide you with a couple of benefits. Most of all they focus the client on user needs, but they also provide you with flexibility about how to fulfil those needs. For example, you could achieve the above through live chat or a bot just as easily as through a traditional checkout process. User story cards don't close down avenues too early in the process.

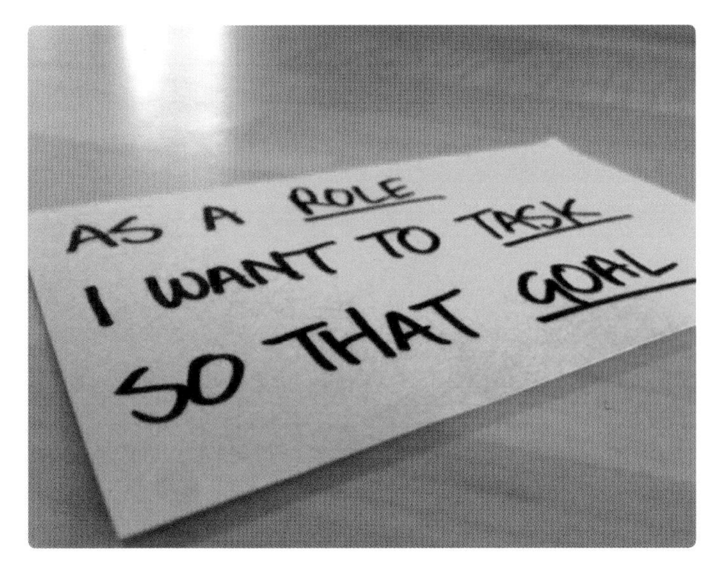

A user story card is a simple tool for focusing colleagues on user needs.

In a typical project you will end up with many user story cards. The exercise of producing these cards will get the client thinking about the user's needs.

Of course, you shouldn't just be thinking about the user's needs. You should be prioritising your work based on them too.

PRIORITISING BASED ON USER NEEDS

No doubt you receive a lot of requests from colleagues. More than you can build. How do you prioritise those projects? How do you decide what gets built and what doesn't?

Chances are, it depends on who's asking. If the CEO wants a project built, it gets built. Your ideas are often at the bottom of the list even though you are the expert in user experience.

In the next chapter I will introduce a policy called digital triage. This aims to prioritise your workload based on some clear criteria, rather than who shouts loudest.

One of those criteria should be user needs. If you want to encourage colleagues to consider user needs then make sure you prioritise work based on those needs.

To do this you will need a prioritised list of audiences. You should prioritise this list based on the value those audiences bring to the business. When new work comes into the department, you need to prioritise it based on which audience it helps. The more important the audience, the faster it will get addressed. This avoids wasting valuable time on unimportant projects.

As you will see in the next chapter, establishing policies for dealing with work is a useful tool in creating the right culture. For now, I just want to mention one other you might want to consider.

ENFORCING USABILITY TESTING

One of the big reasons colleagues aren't thinking about user needs is because they don't interact with users enough. If we want to build a user-centric culture we need to change that.

One area we cannot compromise on is the need to do usability testing as part of any project we work on. But we shouldn't stop there. We should insist that stakeholders attend these sessions.

For example, the UK Government Digital Service has an interesting policy. It says you cannot be a stakeholder in a digital project unless you have been in a user research session within the last six weeks. Now that is one way to get colleagues focused on users!

The UK Government Digital Service requires stakeholders to attend two hours of usability testing every six weeks.

A focus on user needs will make an enormous difference. But it is not the only thing you can do to build a user-centric culture. Another is to make more use of prototypes.

Collaborate Through Prototyping

I have talked a lot about prototyping so far in this book, though I haven't taken the time to define what I consider to be a prototype. Part of the reason for this is that there is no single approach to prototyping.

At its most basic level, a prototype is anything you use to show the proposed nature of a digital product or service. That could be something as simple as a sketch on the back of an envelope or as complex as a working alpha version of a website.

Typically, a prototype will fall somewhere between these two extremes. I'm sure you have produced design comps or wireframes that show how a final product might look. You may also have experimented with storyboarding as a way of explaining a journey through a digital service such as a website.

A prototype can be as simple as a sketch or as complex as a working alpha version of a website.

Although prototyping takes many forms, the benefits it provides are undeniable. If you wish to build a user experience culture, prototyping needs to become the bedrock of your process.

COLLABORATE ON WIREFRAMES

If you wish to reap the full benefit, you cannot produce these prototypes in isolation. The real value of prototyping comes from producing them with stakeholders.

By working on prototypes together you ensure a shared understanding of what the final result will be in a way that is not possible by presenting the prototype to stakeholders. This is because stakeholders will make the decisions needed to create the prototype. Through this process they will learn about the nuances of user experience design. This isn't possible in a presentation.

By working on a prototype, stakeholders will also gain a sense of ownership over the final result. This will make selling the prototype to the rest of the organisation easier. The stakeholders will become advocates for the approach, and they will also have the knowledge to educate colleagues.

Prototyping can also be an excellent way of resolving differences between stakeholders. Visualising ideas helps to bring clarity to these different approaches. Often this is enough to identify the best way forward. Where you need more information, it is straightforward to test these prototypes with users. Creating a culture of testing prototypes will ensure your organisation becomes more user-centric.

Prototyping also encourages experimentation and innovation. Prototypes are cheap to create and the cost of failure is low. You can try an idea and discard it if it does not work. You can explore more potential solutions than you would consider using other methods.

Pushing stakeholders to move beyond their initial ideas is a good way to encourage them to think about user needs.

EXPLORE ALTERNATIVE APPROACHES

One exercise I favour is six-up wireframing. You ask each stakeholder to take a large sheet of paper and fold it in half and then in thirds. This will leave them with six boxes to fill in on the page.

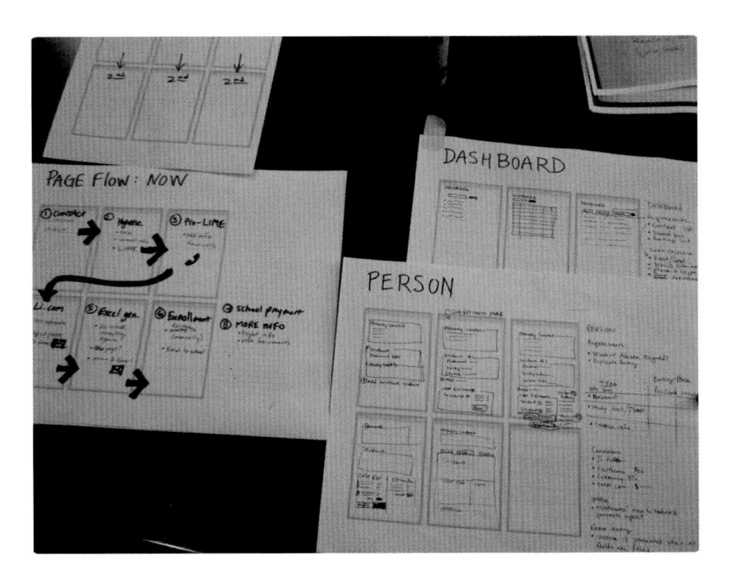

By encouraging colleagues to consider multiple approaches, they will find it easier to think about the needs of users.

You can then ask the stakeholders to wireframe a different solution to the same problem in each of the six boxes. The advantage of this approach is that it forces people to think beyond their initial idea. To explore possibilities that they may not have considered before.

In my experience, they tend to get stuck after one or two alternatives. At this point you can start to encourage them to imagine solutions aimed at different audiences. This is a great way to get them considering the user's perspective, and it still allows them to express their personal preferences in the initial ideas.

A culture of prototyping seems to lead to a culture of user-centric thinking; in most cases the two go hand in hand. But it is not the only way to focus your colleagues on user needs. I also find talking about time as another motivating factor.

Focus On Saving Users' Time

Asking some colleagues to empathise with users can prove quite challenging for them. Not everybody finds empathy easy. This is especially true when they are not having regular contact with the customer.

One way around this problem is to focus not just on the user, but also focus on time.

EXPLAIN WHY TIME MATTERS

For most people in western society, time has become one of our most valuable commodities. Almost all users are too busy. With unprecedented levels of choice, they are unwilling to waste time on any single digital service. If a service does not deliver quickly they will move on to a competitor. As a result, saving users time is the single most important thing you can do to improve the user experience.

Best of all, this is something your colleagues will understand, even if they cannot empathise with your users.

They use other digital services and are just as impatient as your own users. A lack of time is a universal problem we can all relate to.

By talking about time-saving we focus on a tangible metric for improving the user experience, one that our colleagues can understand.

According to Steve Jobs, the slowness of booting the first Mac cost lives.

To get colleagues thinking along these lines I often tell the story of Steve Jobs and the first Macintosh. This is how Andy Hertzfeld, a developer on the original Mac, described events:

One of the things that bothered Steve Jobs the most was the time that it took to boot when the Mac was first powered on. It could take a couple of minutes, or even more, to test memory, initialize the operating system, and load the Finder. One afternoon, Steve came up with an original way to motivate us to make it faster. Larry Kenyon was the engineer working on the disk driver and file system, and one day Steve went into his cubicle and started to exhort him. "The Macintosh boots too slowly. You've got to make it faster!"

Larry started to explain about some of the places where he thought he could improve things, but Steve wasn't interested. He continued, "You know, I've been thinking about it. How many people are going to be using the Macintosh? A million? No, more than that. In a few years, I bet five million people will be booting up their Macintoshes at least once a day.

"Well, let's say you can shave 10 seconds off of the boot time. Multiply that by 5 million users and that's 50 million seconds every single day. Over a year, that's probably dozens of lifetimes. Just think about it. If you make it boot 10 seconds faster, you'll save a dozen lives. That's really worth it, don't you think?"

—Andy Hertzfeld, Revolution in The Valley (2004)

This is a good way to think about time when it comes to user experience. It saves lives.

The problem with talking about time savings is that it can often sound petty. Complaining that a user has to spend a few seconds completing an extra field sounds like a minor inconvenience. But as the story of the first Macintosh shows, a minor inconvenience can become a problem if large numbers of people have to face it.

Also, these minor inconveniences do not exist in isolation. A typical digital service has many such annoyances, from poor performance to badly worded instructions. On their own, these issues are not a big deal; together they become like death by a thousand cuts. It does not take many such inconveniences to drive users away when the competition is so accessible.

Take something as common as slow-loading web pages. Every extra second a user has to wait for a page to load increases the likelihood that they will go elsewhere. According to surveys done by Akamai and Gomez.com,[1] nearly half of web users expect a site to load in two seconds or less. Worse still, they tend to abandon a site that hasn't loaded within three seconds.

1 http://smashed.by/ux48

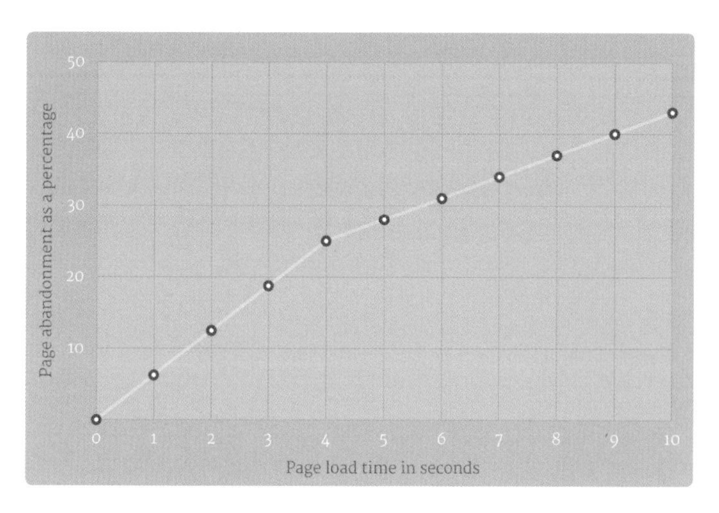

The slower a page takes to load, the higher percentage of people who will abandon your site.

But it is worse than that. Of people using an e-commerce site, 79% said they would not return to a site that was slow, and 44% said they would tell friends about that bad experience.

In short, there is no shortage of evidence to reinforce what your colleagues already know. You cannot afford to waste users' time.

Yet despite the fact that most of us recognise this problem, it is still a common occurrence. That is why you must build a culture of highlighting time-wasters.

HIGHLIGHT TIME WASTERS

Because time is such a powerful way of improving the user experience, it is worth making it a metric for measuring success. Get into the habit of measuring the time it takes a user to complete a task. This will allow you to challenge anything that undermines that metric.

Having a metric such as this will help, though you will still find that colleagues are often unaware of the impact they are having on the time it takes a user to complete a task. For example:

- **Marketers** will often want users to complete extra form fields to allow them to build up a better picture of the customer. They will justify this by saying that they are seeking to improve the customer experience. But having time spent completing a task as a key metric will allow you to combat this.
- **Compliance officers** have requirements around security, terms and conditions, and privacy. Every time they ask a user to give permission or read some legal statement they affect our time metric.
- **Content creators** often write content that is verbose, hard to scan and difficult to read. This increases comprehension time and slows down the user.

- **Developers** probably have the biggest impact on wasting users' time. From passwords to CAPTCHA forms, developers often make their problems the problems of users: problems with spam become a CAPTCHA form that users have to complete; problems with security force users to remember complex passwords. Then, of course, there is the significant impact they have on performance.

CAPTCHA is just one example where we turn our problems into tasks that drain our users' time.

Not that the developers undermined the user experience on purpose. They are often under pressure to deliver on unrealistic timelines and within limited budgets. This forces them to cut corners and compromise the experience.

That is an important thing to remember when talking about time-wasters. Nobody wastes the user's time on purpose. This means it is important not to become accusatory in discussions about time-wasting.

When I introduce the concept of measuring the time it takes a user to complete a task, I do so in a light-hearted way. I turn the metric into a game, a challenge for the team to undertake together. We work together to get that number as low as possible. I have even offered a prize for the person who can come up with the biggest timesaver. You will achieve nothing by alienating your colleagues and creating a culture of confrontation.

Although a focus on saving the user time is important, it shouldn't be our only focus. Another working process that will help build a user-centric culture is a focus on simplicity.

Focus On Simplicity

I have been working in digital for twenty-two years. Not once over all that time have I ever heard somebody suggest that we want to make the user experience more complex. People have always been completely behind the idea of keeping things simple. Why, then, do so many digital projects become complex from a user experience perspective?

The problem is that every stakeholder has needs that add complexity. Once again, we lose simplicity through the collective impact of many small decisions.

If we are going to create a great user experience we need to keep things simple, especially in the early days. By keeping things simple we keep them manageable. It allows us to focus on the key features that are important to users. It helps us keep our priorities straight.

Although our colleagues value simplicity, they do not see that more people means more complexity. We can tell them until we are blue in the face, but no stakeholder is ever going to accept their contributions aren't helpful. We need to show them the problem.

HELP COLLEAGUES SEE COMPLEXITY

The best way to show colleagues the problem is to show users battling with complexity. This will highlight the issue, but it doesn't always drive home the challenges of solving that problem.

What colleagues cannot see is the number of requests that people make on digital services. They cannot see the conflicting requests for content and functionality. We need to expose them to this so they understand the need to compromise.

One way of doing this is called the user attention point exercise. This exercise works best when applied to a particularly complex part of a digital service, like a homepage. Gather all your stakeholders together, all the people who want their content on the homepage of the website. It is important that they see who else is a part of the process so they can see just how many people are contributing complexity.

Split the stakeholders into teams. Get each team to write down all the content or functionality that needs to appear on the homepage. Ask them to be specific and write down as many elements as possible, everything they want to include from the logo to the search box. You can even introduce a competitive component with a prize for the group with the most elements.

With that done, explain to the group that users have limited attention. Some studies suggest that user attention online is less than that of a goldfish, coming in at about 2.7 seconds. This doesn't come as a surprise to people. Like I said, most people know things should be simple. They just don't think it is them who needs to compromise.

To resolve this contradiction, translate user attention into points. Give the group 17 points of user attention. It doesn't need to be 17, but in my experience this is about right. Too few points and colleagues will find the task impossible;

too many and it's not a realistic representation of users' limited attention.

Now get them to spend those points on whatever elements they wish to include on the page. Anything included on the page has to be assigned at least one point of user attention. If they want users to pay more attention to one element over another, it needs more attention points. For example, a carousel would require many more points than an element in the footer.

You will find this exercise forces the stakeholders to compromise. But you are not done yet. Inevitably they will spread their points thinly, rarely spending more than one or two points on a single item.

By comparing the Google and Yahoo homepages it becomes obvious that stakeholders need to focus user attention.

Once they have completed the exercise, show them the Google and Yahoo homepages. Ask the group which is more user-friendly. I can tell you from experience nobody ever says Yahoo.

Explain that Google is more effective because it has spent the majority of users' attention points on the search box. Yahoo, by contrast, has spread its points. Now is the time to point out to the group that they have created the Yahoo homepage by spreading their points too thinly.

This is usually a lightbulb moment for most groups. They realise that they have compromised the experience to cram as many elements on to the page as possible. But for good measure, get them to repeat the exercise with this new knowledge. You will find they make better decisions and cut everything but the most essential elements.

An exercise like this will prove invaluable when designing a digital service. But it isn't so effective for simplifying an existing service. For that we need the laws of simplicity.

MAKING LEGACY SIMPLE

A book of the same name by John Maeda inspired my laws of simplicity. This excellent book gives solid advice on how to make any system, product or service simpler. For our purposes we are going to simplify his already simple book even further.

The Laws of Simplicity by John Maeda provides an excellent method for simplifying any system, product or service.

Giving colleagues a structure within which to work helps bring clarity to complex discussions. The laws of simplicity are one example of this.

When faced with redesigning a part of an existing digital service we apply the laws of simplicity. We look at each element within that part of the service and pass it through the following steps.

1. **Can we remove this element?** If we did, what difference would it make to the service? Would it damage the experience or improve it? Who would it damage the experience for and are they a key audience?

2. **If we cannot remove the element, can we hide it?** Could we move this item deeper into the service so that it has less visibility and does not distract from more important tasks? For example, on a website, we could move it deeper into the site's information architecture. This is a useful approach for functionality that serves secondary audiences.

3. **If we cannot hide the element, could we shrink it?** Could you reduce its prominence within the user interface so it does not distract from more important things? For example, could we make it smaller or change the colour? This works well for less important functionality that serves a primary audience.

You will find that the remove, hide or shrink mantra is a great way to focus colleagues on simplifying the experience. It is so effective, in fact, that you will find colleagues latching on to it. They will start referring to the principle without you prompting.

There is a general lesson to learn from this simple mantra. A good way of embedding user experience best practice in an organisation is to encapsulate it in a digestible form.

We have a tendency to make user experience design sound complicated, perhaps as an attempt to establish its worth. But in so doing we make it hard to grasp. Instead, we should condense it into easily remembered nuggets. That is what we tried to do with our common vision back in chapter 3. Phrases like 'Decide with data' or 'Launch is just the start' take user experience concepts and present them in a memorable form which encourages repetition and will spread them throughout the organisation.

Another example is 'Always be iterating', a phrase that is a fundamental principle for building around user needs and one that embraces the idea of starting simple.

Always Be Iterating

I stared in horror at the Gantt chart laid out before me. I have never been a huge fan of Gantt charts, but this one was in a league of its own. It was so big that Neil, the project manager, had laid it out on the boardroom table.

The Gantt chart was for the redesign and relaunch of a major website. The complexity of it didn't surprise me as this project was a major undertaking. My problem was that Neil felt confident enough to create a timeline like this. A timeline that laid out in detail every piece of functionality we would build. Every nuance of the project. To my mind, we just didn't understand enough about what users needed to be able to even guess at what the functionality would be. How could he define it in black and white like that at this stage?

You cannot plan a digital service like a traditional physical project.

This is a common problem I see all the time: project managers trying to specify and plan for a digital project in the same way they would deliver a physical one. This is a problem because delivering a digital experience is nothing like a traditional project.

In traditional projects you would create a detailed plan before even beginning to build anything. When you do start building, rarely would you consider deviating from that original plan. The specification and Gantt chart are the definitive roadmap.

Imagine for a moment you are a car manufacturer planning to launch a new model. This is a major investment for you. You need to design the car, build prototypes, test and create an entire new production line. The investment in materials, people and systems is huge.

The problem with this is that it is a big risk. Once that car hits the market there is no going back. People will either love it or hate it. But you cannot turn back. You have made the investment.

Admittedly, you will have done some market research. People have said they are willing to buy the car. But saying something and doing it are two different things. What if it gets a bad review? What if the economy takes a dip? What if you missed something in the production and it is defective in some way?

In such a situation it is not surprising that people plan projects in immense detail. The risk is huge and careful planning up front minimises that risk. But digital projects are different for two reasons.

First, digital projects have a low cost of failure. If something goes wrong the cost of fixing it – even after launch – is low. You cannot update every car you have sold, but you can update a digital service. This allows for a lot more experimentation.

Second, digital services provide continual user feedback. You know far more about consumer behaviour than a car manufacturer would.

These two factors allow you to take a different approach. It allows you to build minimum viable products.

MINIMUM VIABLE PRODUCT

If we presume that we don't know what users want until we show them, then this changes the way we work. If we can adapt as we build and gather feedback on user needs, we will find ourselves starting projects from a different premise.

Gone is the need for lengthy specification processes. Gone is the need for long lists of features. All we need to do is identify the core of our service. At the most basic level, what will it do?

You can see this at work with the digital services you use every day. Take Twitter. When Twitter launched it did just one thing. You could post 140 characters to your followers. That was it.

Twitter started with a minimum viable product which has evolved over time based on user behaviour.

Today, Twitter offers many more features. You can reply to people, add photos, send direct messages and more. These features were added as Twitter watched how people used the service. People started to use the @ symbol when they wanted to reply to another person, so they built that into the platform. People shared links to images and so Twitter added the ability to post images.

But in its early days, Twitter was basic. It was a minimum viable product. It was as simple as it could be and still remain useful.

The great thing about this approach is that you can get to market fast. What is more, you keep your initial investment down until you know what people want. It also helps users grasp the core of your service before overwhelming them with information or features.

A minimum viable product is also a great tool for getting colleagues and management on board with user-centric design. They love the fact that they get to see results fast. They also love that it minimises risk and investment.

But it also provides a chance to educate them about the need for continual investment in the experience, encouraging a move away from the cycle of redesign every few years – a wasteful cycle that involves throwing out what you built before and starting from scratch, all because the digital service hasn't kept up with changing organisational and user needs.

When talking about a minimum viable product, you make it clear this is the beginning of a process. You always talk about the next feature and the next stage. You move away from the idea that one day this project will end and you will have finished the website or mobile app.

A minimum viable product also focuses on designing with data. The whole idea of it is to observe how users interact with it and adapt. Decisions become driven by data on user needs, not the whims of stakeholders. It changes what drives your digital direction from being internally driven to externally focused.

Not that this will stop stakeholders coming up with ideas. But instead of the executive forcing you to build those ideas, you now have the option to test them. You can create a small prototype or minimum viable product, something you can test with real users and then let the data speak for itself. This avoids the need to tell colleagues their idea stinks!

Of course, even building a minimum viable product needs managing. This is where it would be tempting to go scurrying back to our Gantt charts. Instead, we should apply the principles of iteration to each stage of building our product, so we can gather even more user feedback and build a more appropriate service.

HOW TO ITERATE

At its core, iteration is a simple process. You form a hypothesis around what you think users want and build a prototype. You then test that prototype and observe how users respond to it. Based on what you observe, you iterate, improving the prototype. You then test again and keep iterating until you are ready to launch.

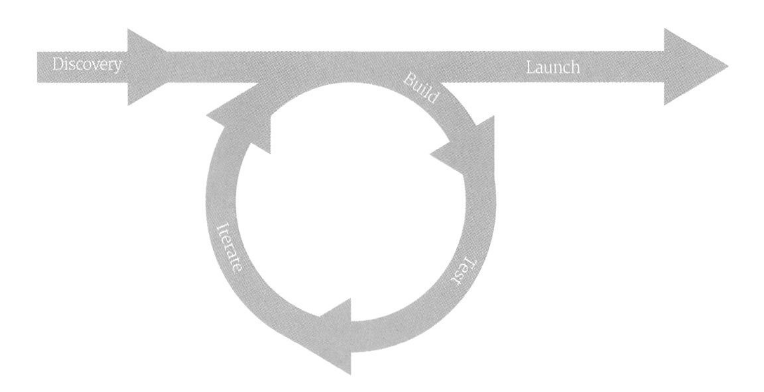

Iteration is a cyclic process.

We can apply this principle of continual iteration to an entire digital service or a single feature. The important part is testing with real users. The idea of iteration embeds testing into the heart of your process. It refocuses the organisation around building using user data.

When designing an entire digital service, it can also be helpful to break down development into a series of stages. These stages make management easier, and they also focus colleagues on building around user needs.

Discovery Phase

Stage one is a discovery phase. This short stage is where you research your users' needs for using the service and establish how you measure success. It is also where you seek to understand any constraints for the service, be they technological or policy related.

Alpha Phase
Following the discovery phase, the service moves into an alpha phase. This is a short phase where you prototype solutions for user needs. In this phase you test with a small group of users and stakeholders. This will allow you to gather early feedback on the service.

Beta Phase
Once you are confident in the alpha, it is time to move into the beta phase. This is the version of the service that will go live when it is complete.

At some point in the beta phase you can make it available to a wider audience. For example, a website might sit alongside the existing site on a separate subdomain. You can encourage users to kick the tyres of the beta and provide feedback. This allows you to see the service's effectiveness with a bigger group of users.

Live Phase
When the beta is more effective than the existing service (if one exists) you can launch the service. In doing so, you replace what went before.

But work does not stop at this point. Instead, you continue to iterate the service based on observations of users interacting with it. It is these post-launch improvements that have the biggest impact on the service. I have worked on digital services where a single post-launch tweak increased the conversion rate by 6%, all by observing users struggling with the interaction and testing possible solutions.

This principle of continual incremental improvement of a digital service is at the heart of good user experience design. From speaking to employees at Booking.com and Amazon I can tell you they are running over a hundred tests at any one time. When it comes to user experience, there is always room for improvement.

Sites like Booking.com are constantly iterating and improving their services by watching user behaviour.

Introducing the right working practices will go a long way to improving the user experience. It will also start to change organisational culture.

Through prototyping, iteration and minimum viable products you will show the power of user experience design. This will help win over management. As they begin to understand the potential they will want to embed it at every level of the business. They will want to become a real customer-centric organisation. But desiring it and achieving it are two different things.

Transform The Organisational Culture

It is time that we live up to our commitment to our customers. The customer experience is our number one aim for the coming year. We ask you to do everything it takes to place the customer's needs at the heart of your work."

If you are anything like me your heart would soar if you read a company-wide email like that from your senior management team. Finally you have the support needed to bring about real change. Finally your company will be a user-centric organisation.

I was fortunate enough to work with an organisation whose senior management team sent out such an email. They made it clear that customer experience was their number one goal. Yet, a year on and little had changed, despite countless initiatives and training sessions. Any momentum gathered had stalled despite the best intentions of management. What had gone wrong?

The problem was one of culture and structure. The company didn't have the right culture. It also lacked the right organisational framework to deliver on the new mandate from management.

The grass-roots approach to user experience will take you so far; managerial support will take you even further. But sooner or later somebody will need to address the shape of the business. The time will come to reorient the entire organisation around the customer.

Of course, restructuring your company is not your job and isn't likely to become so. This falls to the senior management team. But when the time comes they will need your help. They will need advice on where to begin.

I know this sounds intimidating. But the chances are it is someway off and not something you need to worry about right now. Even when the time does come, you can start small. You can begin by encouraging cross-departmental collaboration.

Work Across Silos

As we established right back in chapter 1, the customer experience spans departments. As a result we need close collaboration between those departments. Unfortunately, in many organisations that kind of close collaboration does not exist. Each department has its own area of responsibility. Other than limited hand-off points, they fail to work together.

Restructuring those departmental silos is a major undertaking that could take years. It will also need a lot of managerial support. But starting out can be simple enough and done on an informal basis. You can simply start approaching, and collaborating with, other teams.

You might think you already do that, but do you? Collaboration is not the same as forming a committee and holding meetings. Collaboration should be about working together, not talking together. It should be about sitting side by side, working on solutions at the same time. What is more, you can do exactly that right now. There is nothing stopping you.

Collaboration can be as simple as getting up from your desk and going to sit next to somebody who you should be working with on a project. Maybe you are working on a micro-site for an upcoming marketing campaign. Pick up your laptop and go and sit with the marketing team.

This is something that email marketing company MailChimp encourages. Empty desks are scattered around the office to make it easy for people to up sticks and move to sit next to people from other teams. Games company Valve goes a step further by issuing every member of staff a desk on wheels. Employees are encouraged to wheel their desks over to colleagues they want to work with.

The offices of games company Valve have desks that can be moved around to encourage collaboration.

This simple first step is powerful. If you are sitting next to stakeholders you can show them your work as you go and ask them questions. This engages them in the process and gives them a sense of ownership over the final result. Most of all it begins to build a relationship and gives you an opportunity to introduce them to user-centric thinking.

Of course, if you have many stakeholders across more than one department this isn't going to work to any great extent. But that doesn't mean we have to resort to a committee meeting.

Among the most powerful ways of encouraging cross-departmental collaboration are workshops. Instead of getting people into a room to discuss the user experience, get people into a room to start building that experience.

Use workshops to start prototyping solutions to a user need, rather than discussing what it should do. Let's imagine you are building a mobile app for the company. Instead of holding a meeting to discuss features, run a workshop to wireframe key screens, or try creating a storyboard of the user journey within the app.

One of the problems with meetings is that people can go away with different interpretations of the discussion. Workshops, on the other hand, ensure everybody ends up with a shared understanding of how the app will work - they can see what they will get at the end.

Although workshops are a great way of gaining a shared understanding, they do have their limits, the biggest of which is the fact they do nothing to expose participants to users. There is a danger that the group will prototype a solution that does not fulfil user needs.

You can mitigate this risk by making it clear that anything prototyped in the workshop must then be tested with users. In an ideal world, workshop participants would attend the test sessions so they can observe the results. If that is not possible, record the sessions and arrange a second workshop. This will allow participants to watch edited highlights and amend their approach.

The more you can get stakeholders involved in the process, the better. If time allows, you might even want to consider a design sprint.

A design sprint[1] is a method for prototyping with stakeholders, popularised by Google Ventures.[2] It is a five-day process of design, prototyping, and testing ideas with customers. You can use it to engage stakeholders in generating solutions to user experience challenges that you can then test. In only a week you can brainstorm ideas, narrow down to possible solutions, and prototype those solutions. You can then test those solutions with real customers, all while engaging colleagues from across the organisation.

It is a great way of encouraging collaboration. It will also allow you to educate colleagues about user needs and user experience design best practice.

If you are considering running a design sprint, I would recommend Jake Knapp's (Google Ventures) book on the subject.

1 http://smashed.by/ux49
2 http://smashed.by/ux50

The typical design sprint runs from Monday to Friday.

You will spend Monday mapping out the problem and picking an important place to focus your efforts. In the morning the team and the primary decision maker will agree a long-term goal to aim for. Next, you will map out the challenge you wish to solve. In the afternoon you will ask experts across the company to share their experience. Finally, you will pick a target for the week: an ambitious but manageable piece of the problem you are trying to solve.

Tuesday is about exploring a variety of possible solutions. The day will start by finding inspiration and discussing how you could improve on that inspiration. In the afternoon each person will sketch possible solutions. This will emphasise critical thinking over artistic quality.

On Wednesday you will pick the best solution and turn your ideas into a testable hypothesis. In the morning you will discuss the different solutions people came up with. The decision maker will decide which ones have the best chance of achieving the long-term goal. In the afternoon you will take the winning solutions and turn them into a storyboard. This will be a step-by-step plan for your prototype.

On Thursday you will work together to create a high-fidelity prototype. This will be a realistic facade to test with customers. It maybe smoke and mirrors behind the scenes, but it will look realistic to users. This is what will allow you to build a prototype in just one day.

Finally, on Friday you will interview users and test the prototype with real customers. This will establish whether your solution works in the real world.

A design sprint is a great way to kick off any large project. Not only does it help find a viable approach, it also encourages collaboration that starts to break down the departmental silos and encourage cooperation.

But although collaboration is a great start, in the end it will not be enough to become a customer-centric organisation. For that, senior management will need to address the underlying structures of the business.

Address Organisational Structure

You do not need to change organisational structures overnight. Doing so would be damaging to the business and the user experience. Instead, we need to establish a roadmap for change that the business can support and allows colleagues to adapt.

This roadmap takes the typical organisation through three stages.

DECENTRALISED BEGINNINGS

In my experience, organisations begin their journey towards a user-centric structure with a decentralised and chaotic approach. As we have discussed, there will be people within departments trying to improve the user experience, but very little joined-up thinking, and these individuals often feel isolated and alone. Worst of all, there is often a lot of replication of effort, especially in the area of user research.

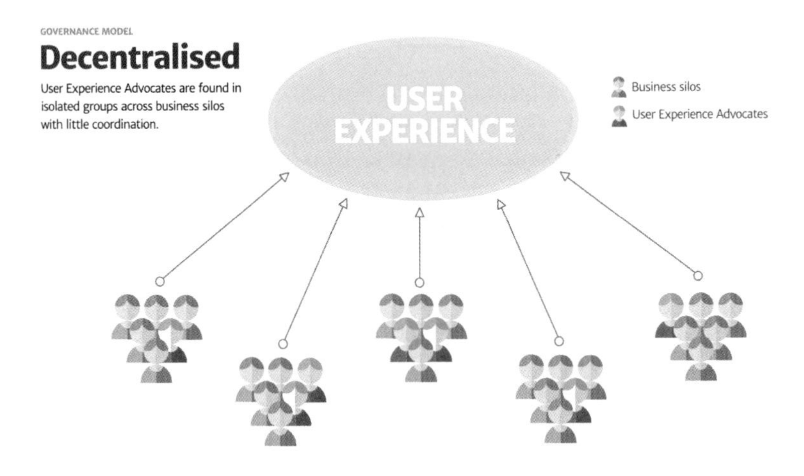

The first step is to coordinate these people through our user experience mailing list. Just getting these people talking is a good start. In time, we can get them working together on specific projects by forming cross disciplinary teams.

However, organisations at this stage in the journey are still operating in the dark ages of user experience. They are immature in their approach. The only way to bring order to the chaos is to centralise.

CENTRALISE TO STANDARDISE

It is tempting to establish a distributed model of managing user experience from day one. But this would be a mistake. It will be hard for a new culture to get established when diluted across the entire company. It will also be difficult to establish standards and approaches between such disparate groups. Instead, we need first to centralise.

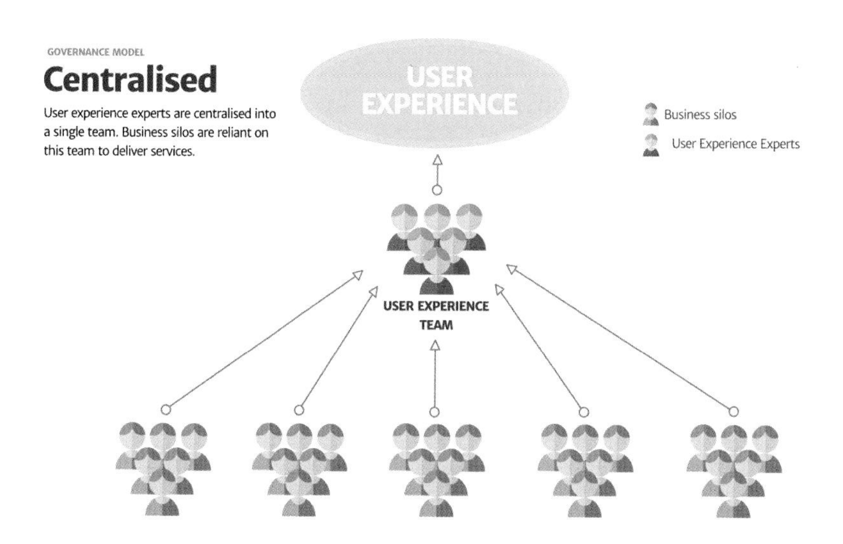

By creating a group dedicated to improving the user experience, you can set standards and establish a new culture. Where this team sits in the organisation is irrelevant. What matters is that it has an executive sponsor who values user experience, someone who will protect the culture of the new team from the rest of the organisation.

Think of this team as an innovation centre, a place where senior management can introduce a new working method and a different way of doing business. A place that implements all the principles talked about in the last few chapters. A place protected from the politics of the rest of the company.

But management must be careful. This department could become another business silo, isolating user experience within the company. Many digital teams I work with find themselves trapped in this position. They are doing great work, but it never goes anywhere. It doesn't change the organisation.

To address this problem it is important to establish straight away the department's mandate as being educational. Too many teams of this type perceive their job as being to deliver services to users. This will be part of their role, but it is not the primary reason for their existence.

The trouble is that no single team can provide an outstanding user experience by themselves. It has to be a cross-departmental effort. Any team tasked with this job has to transform the rest of the organisation to be user-centric. Their primary goal has to be education.

We have already covered in this book many ways of doing this. Ultimately, nothing beats working side by side with colleagues from other departments.

Whenever your user experience team (or whatever you call them) works on a project they should have a service owner as part of the team. This is somebody from the department who owns the service you are building.

This person should be working on the service with you day in and day out. They will attend testing with users, see best practice in action, and experience the culture of the team.

When they return to their own department they will take this new culture with them. Like a virus they will infect their team with this new culture and way of thinking. With your support they will begin to change attitudes within their team.

As other departments begin to grasp user experience best practice, the central team can begin to hand back control to them. Departments can start to manage their own digital services with support from the centre. That is when the organisation begins to shift to the final stage, a collaborative model.

ESTABLISH A COLLABORATIVE MODEL

I don't believe the need for a central user experience team will ever go away. You will always need a team to establish standards and coordinate between departments.

You will also need to have a central team for developing tools that all the departments can use. For example, the UK Government Digital Service is developing a platform of tools that different government departments can use on the individual services they build.

That said, as understanding of user experience design increases, departments can take more control.

In the end you will have user experience specialists operating in almost every department. A central team will coordinate their activities, but how this team manages people will vary. However, a matrix management approach is often the best way forward.

IBM recently invested $100 million in user experience design. This included the recruitment of over 1,000 designers. They have also built ten new interaction experience labs.

What I find most interesting about IBM's approach is how they manage all those new designers.[3] IBM has realised that these designers need to work within all the departments across the company. They also know that to do their job they need support from people who understand design principles.

With that in mind, they have established a matrix management structure. User experience professionals work in teams across the company, and report into the central design function. This ensures that designers are working with colleagues across the organisation while maintaining the design culture through contact with their line manager.

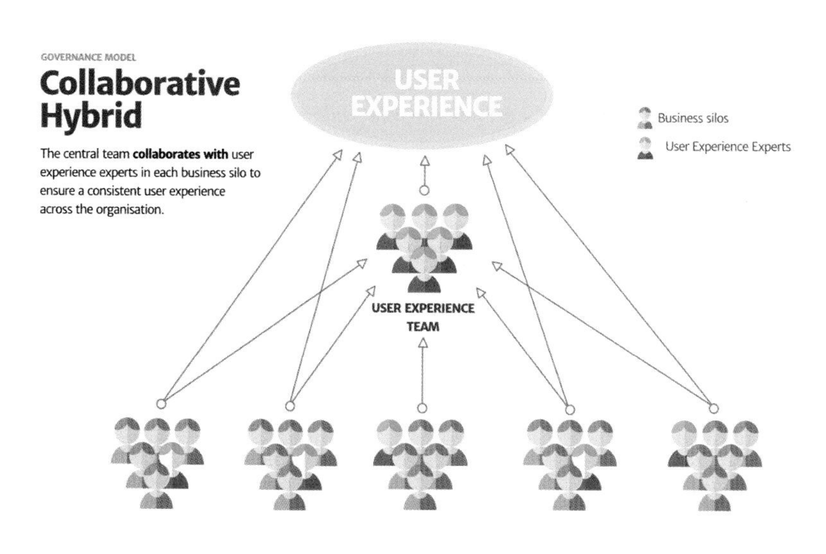

3 http://smashed.by/ux51

This overcomes the biggest problem with embedding user experience professionals in a department. They end up delivering the whims of their line manager, rather than what is best for the user. But when you do not report into the department, it provides more freedom to deliver what users need, not what the manager wants.

This matrix management approach ensures there is a champion of user experience in every part of the business. It also ensures those people get support from a central team. With this kind of structure you will find user-centric thinking becomes embedded into the company's psyche.

KEEP MOVING FORWARD

Where your organisation is on this journey will vary. You may still be in the dark ages of user experience or you may have established a central team. You may even be transitioning from one stage to the next.

Wherever you are, the key is to keep pushing forward. As I said earlier, discourage management from leapfrogging stages. But also fix their eyes on the end goal which is to integrate user experience at every level of the business. Restructuring to include user experience experts across the business will make a big difference. But a lack of focus on user experience is not just a structural issue. It is also a cultural one.

Organisations have an inherent personality. Every organisation is different and it can be hard to pin down where that culture has come from. Often it can hold back the adoption of user experience principles. Nowhere is that more evident than in its attitude towards failure.

Break The Fear Of Failure

Deep rooted within the culture of many organisations is a fear of making mistakes. People are afraid that if they mess up, management will reprimand or even fire them.

This is understandable in situations where mistakes are expensive. When the stakes are high it is important to emphasise the cost of errors. Remember my car manufacturing example from earlier? An error in the design of a car may well be enough to sink the whole company. No wonder many companies are so risk-averse and employees so terrified of messing up.

But as we know, digital has a low cost of failure. It is easy to adapt and learn from mistakes. In fact, digital services improve through failure and experimentation. This means that a culture of fear around failure can be damaging. Breaking a culture of fear around failure is a tough nut to crack. Even when management encourages people not to fear failure, staff are often sceptical. I have heard employees argue that although management say they are OK with failure, they aren't really. It is just too deep-rooted in the culture to believe that things have changed.

Management needs to lead by example on this one. They need to highlight their own failures. Tim Chen, CEO of NerdWallet, set up a fail wall in their office. This wall is covered with Post-it notes where people have shared their failures. Crucially, Tim himself is a regular contributor. One of his Post-it notes reads:

I tried to outsource PR to an agency, idea generation and all. We got five press hits in six months."

This kind of honest admission of failure by management shifts the culture to one of experimentation.

Another way to address the fear of failure is to laugh about it. At the digital agency I ran for thirteen years we had a muppet award. We gave this cuddly toy to anybody who messed up. The muppet award became a standing joke and moved from desk to desk as different people made mistakes. By joking about failure, it became less intimidating and less fear surrounded it. I have the honour of winning the muppet of the year award for six years in succession!

Consider creating a fail wall where together you openly share your failures.

There is also a serious underlying point to failure. We are not celebrating failure as much as we are celebrating experimentation. Failure is an inevitable side effect of experimentation and it also has value in its own right – failure provides more information: information that helps you improve.

This is a fundamental principle of scientific research and it is worth reminding colleagues of that. You don't find a new treatment for Alzheimers or a revolutionary propulsion system on your first try! You carry out a series of experiments and learn from each iteration. That is exactly what we should be doing when building digital services. The more we experiment and fail, the more we learn and the higher the chance we will get it right next time.

Of course, failure does carry a cost, even in the digital field. We don't want to make unnecessary mistakes. One client of mine had a great phrase which I have come to adopt as a mantra of sorts:

Only make new mistakes."

Introducing that kind of thinking will create a culture ripe for improving the user experience.

But for a culture of experimentation to flourish, management needs to change the way your organisation funds user experience.

Make UX An Operational Expense

When it comes to business there are two basic costs: capital expenditure and operational expenses.

Capital expenditure is money an organisation spends to buy fixed assets, like a building or equipment. An operational expense is money spent on the ongoing running of the business. This often involves things like wages or rent.

Too often management see digital services that support the user's experience as a capital cost. Instead, they should see it as an operational one. In the eyes of management and finance you buy a website, content management system or some other digital asset.

In essence, they see digital like purchasing a building. You buy it and then spend a small amount on ongoing maintenance. Yet it is more like planting a garden. Yes, there is an initial outlay, but there is also significant ongoing investment in that garden to reach maturity. Planting the garden is only the start.

The idea that digital is a capital expense comes from how we have dealt with websites in the past. We have redesigned our sites every few years and then abandoned them in the intervening time. This made sense in the past when websites were little more than brochures. But when a website becomes business critical, this thinking fails for three reasons:

- Periodic redesign is wasteful.
- We only understand user needs post-launch.
- We waste money and time building unwanted features.

Let's unpack those a little more:

1. PERIODIC REDESIGN IS WASTEFUL

The traditional pattern of redesign is wasteful. Every few years, an organisation decides to relaunch its website. They launch the website and then abandon it except for some minor content updates. Over time, the design looks dated, the technology unfit for purpose and the content incorrect.

In the end, the website becomes an embarrassment and the company stops referring people to it. Management then intervenes and commissions a redesign. But by this point it is too late. For a significant part of its life the website has not been fit for purpose.

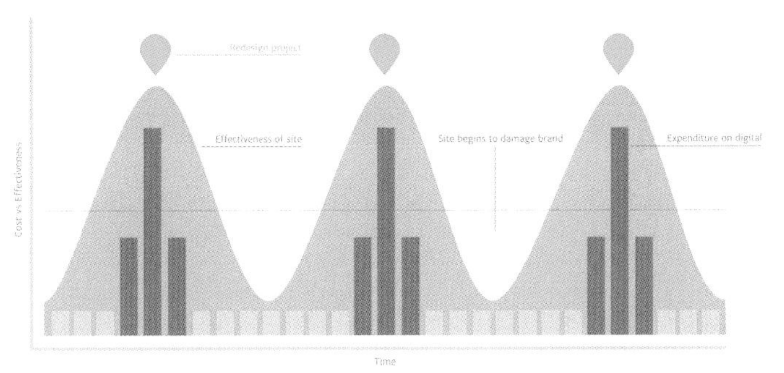

Periodic redesign every few years means your website is ineffective for a considerable portion of its life.

When we do finally redesign our site, we replace the whole thing. We do this despite some elements of it still being serviceable. It is like buying a house, failing to clean it, and buying a new one when it becomes dirty! Although I confess

I would like to do this if I could afford it – I hate housework.

2. WE ONLY UNDERSTAND USER NEEDS POST-LAUNCH

But the waste does not stop there. We build features into our websites that are not needed. This is because we only understand what users want after we have launched the site.

No amount of research replaces seeing real users interacting with a real website. That means we only understand if we have got things right once we have launched the website. Unfortunately, this is exactly the same moment the money dries up if management sees digital as a capital expense.

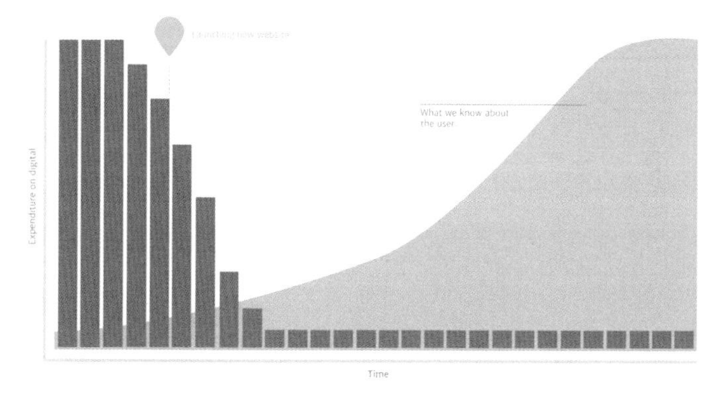

It is not until the money dries up that we really begin to understand users' needs.

The site goes live and everybody walks away.

3. WE WASTE MONEY AND TIME BUILDING UNWANTED FEATURES

We know that we don't understand users' needs until after we launch. That is why we need to create a minimum viable product. We allow the user to shape the digital services we provide by launching a basic service and then responding to feedback.

But when management sees digital as a capital expense this is impossible. Capital expenditure turns our digital service into a project, rather than an ongoing investment. Projects need fixed budgets and that means fixed specifications, which are a best guess of what users want. At worst, they are a wish list of what the company would like to build. This means that organisations over-engineer their digital services. It is typical for organisations to add features they believe they might want in the future, or features they guess users might find useful. It is all guesswork.

Instead, organisations should build the core of a digital service. They should then evolve it based on user feedback and changes in organisational requirements. This is much more cost-effective.

We have covered this already. But if management continues to treat digital services as a capital expense it will not happen. For your organisation to become user-centric it needs to move to a model that has an ongoing investment in user experience. The boom and bust cycle of redesigns needs to end.

If user experience gets the regular funding it needs, it opens up the chance to do more than building and maintaining digital services. The organisation can start addressing the policy issues that undermine the user experience.

Update Policies And Procedures

Back in chapter 3 we put together a set of principles around which we could build our user experience culture. To help you get started I provided a sample list of possible principles to include. One of those principles read as follows:

While endeavouring to meet the needs of consumers we will encounter organisational roadblocks, from IT policy and branding guidelines to compliance issues and financial policy. Instead of accepting these constraints we need to question them. Just because a constraint made sense in the past does not mean it does so now. The organisation needs to question whether the constraint is worth the cost to the user experience.

At the time, I didn't go into any more depth about why I included this in the list. But policies and procedures will have a huge influence over whether a culture of user experience thrives or dies.

If your business is pre-digital, the policies it has will not be compatible with the needs of connected consumers. As a result they will hinder more than they help. This is because policy can be a dangerous thing.

THE PROBLEM WITH POLICY

Companies have policies about everything from hiring contractors to what software you can install. They have policies around compliance and communication, procurement and pricing.

The problem with policy is that we tend to blindly accept it. We feel it is unmovable. This is especially true when those policies come from outside the business. I work with some clients in the financial sector who are closely regulated. All companies have legal obligations around things like data protection or privacy. These kinds of policies we see as set in stone. Yet they aren't as black and white as you might think.

Policies and regulation are almost always open to interpretation. Take, for example, the European legislation on the use of cookies. This says that you need to inform users if your website tracks them using cookies.

On the surface this seems pretty black and white. But is it really? What does it mean to inform the user? Does the user have to say they agree or can you just show a warning?

How prominent does the notice have to be? The rules do not specify. This means each organisation has to decide how it is going to interpret the legislation.

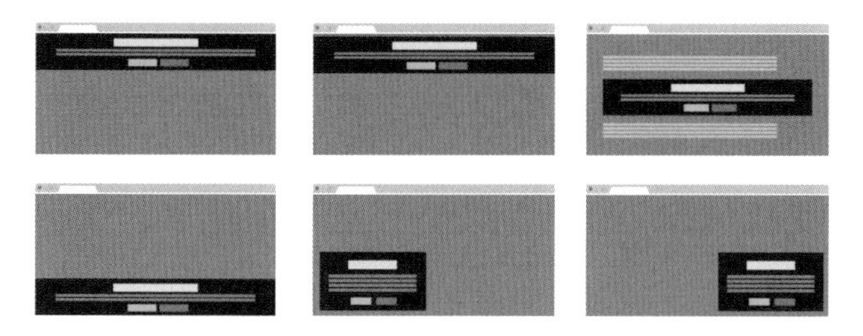

There are many ways to meet regulatory requirements such as European cookie legislation. Who is to say which way is correct?

If you work within a large organisation you may have a compliance team, a group of people whose job it is to make sure the organisation complies with policies and procedures. In smaller organisations it tends to be the responsibility of managers across the company. In either case, these people are interpreting policies. They have to decide how the organisation will follow them, both internal and external.

This need to interpret policy issues means we do not need to accept them blindly, even when they are a legal obligation. There is a discussion to be had around how to interpret them, a discussion that can include the needs of users. This is yet one more reason why we need to start breaking down departmental silos. We must start working with colleagues across our organisation, including compliance.

Policies can be dangerous when applied indiscriminately or allowed to become out of date. But not all policies are bad. In fact, we can use policies to help shape a more user-centric culture.

THE POTENTIAL OF POLICY

We can use the fact that people tend to accept policies without question to our advantage. If we can enshrine user experience best practice as company policy, it is much more likely to stick. That is because policy shapes culture, for better or worse.

Having policies around user experience makes a lot of sense. Not only does it help shape culture, it also establishes standard operating procedures.

How much time have you wasted having the same arguments again and again? Arguments over prioritisation of work, maintenance of content, or what appears on the homepage. We waste so much time going over the same old ground. If you establish policies to address these issues then you only need to make the argument once.

You will also find it easier to establish a policy than to fight individual battles. That is because a policy is a debate about a strategic approach, not a specific application.

Imagine going to a colleague and saying that you intend to remove their content from the website. I bet you would have a fight on your hands. But what if you asked them to support a policy which said content failing to generate a certain amount of traffic will get archived? That would be easier. The result may well be the same, but a policy is abstract. You are asking for agreement to a principle, not targeting their specific content.

That is another good thing about policy, it isn't personal. When you tell somebody you are going to remove their content, it comes across as a personal attack on them and their content. If you say no to their request for a link on the homepage, that will turn into a confrontation. A policy isn't personal. You apply it to all. You aren't the one saying no or removing the content. You are just implementing an agreed policy that applies to everybody without favouritism.

Policy is a great way of avoiding politics and decision-making based on ego. It is a great way of putting the user first without getting sucked into endless debates. So what policies should you consider?

EXAMPLES OF POLICY

When deciding on policy, start by looking at areas you find yourself talking about a lot: things about user experience best practice that people don't understand, or issues around current culture. These are often good candidates for establishing a policy.

What policies you put in place within your organisation will depend on your culture. Here are four policies that I often find myself recommending.

HOMEPAGE PLACEMENT

In many organisations, whose content gets to go on the homepage is a hot topic. The fact that most users don't arrive via the homepage won't make any difference. The result is a homepage so cluttered with content competing for attention that users cannot find anything.

A policy is one way to reduce this problem. Establish a limited number of content slots on the homepage and have a policy for deciding what appears in these slots.

For example, if somebody wants their content on the homepage, the policy might say it needs to earn that right. You do this by first placing it in a universal footer. This means the content is on every page of the website, although in a less prominent position. If it can outperform an existing homepage element in traffic it replaces that element on the homepage.

The University of Surrey website is a good example of how a footer can be used to test the performance of content before promoting it to the homepage.

This policy avoids you having to say no to any homepage content requests. You just apply the policy. And the entire policy favours content that users want, enforcing a user experience culture.

CONTENT MANAGEMENT

The management of content is another area crying out for some well-written policies. As Kristina Halvorson points out in her book on content strategy, websites have become full of redundant, out-of-date and trivial content. This makes it hard for users to find the content they care about. Yet people do not manage the content they put online. They do not remove it when it is no longer needed.

To reduce this problem, create a policy around content archiving. Maybe you'll archive content if it fails to reach a certain threshold of traffic; or you might archive it if the content creator hasn't reviewed it within a set period. Whatever you decide, have a criterion that triggers the application of the policy.

What archiving looks like will vary between organisations. You can tailor your policy depending on the kind of pushback you get. Some people may argue that although their content gets low traffic it is important to a critical audience. Your policy can then say that content isn't deleted, but removed from navigation and search. This will still allow people to find the content from search engines, and the content owner to give out the web address.

How you structure the policy is up to you. The point is that it will reduce the amount of clutter users have to wade through to find what they care about.

By establishing a policy for archiving content you will avoid endless debates every time you want to remove content.

PRIORITISATION POLICY

The most important area to establish a policy in is how you prioritise the digital services you work on. No doubt you have lots of colleagues suggesting digital services you should build. Often the order you build these projects comes down to who shouts loudest and who is the most senior.

Of course, this does nothing to build a user-centric culture, as user needs don't feature in the decision-making. A policy can correct this discrepancy by building user needs into the prioritisation process.

One approach I recommend is allocating work a score that decides how high on your task list a work package gets placed. The higher the score, the higher in the list and the faster it gets built.

As new work comes in you should give it a score and place it in the appropriate place in the queue. This means that work with a low score may never make it to the top of the list as new work comes in with a higher score. This has the advantage that you never need to say no to an idea. You just give it a low score and it will never reach the head of the queue.

Of course, you cannot just make up the score – you need agreed criteria for scoring work. Because we are trying to build a user-centric culture make sure user needs are the primary criterion. For example, work packages that fulfil a high priority need of an important audience would score well. Work on an edge case wouldn't rate as highly.

User needs don't need to be the only scoring criteria. You could also score based on business goals or return on investment.

A policy like this will transform how your organisation works. It will focus colleagues on user needs and ensure equality across the organisation. It will also allow you to submit your own ideas for work packages so you are not reduced to building the ideas of others. Because the policy is impartial, you are less likely to receive criticism for favouring your own ideas.

USER INTERACTION

Finally, I want to address one of the biggest challenges of building a user experience culture. How do you get colleagues to spend time with users?

Without doubt, the best way of building a user experience culture is to ensure colleagues spend time with users. The sad truth is most people in organisations don't have a lot of contact with the customer. This is especially true the higher in the organisation you go. Unless senior management are spending time with users, how can you build a user experience culture?

Of course, as you follow the advice in this book your colleagues will be more enthusiastic about the idea. But it is easy for this to get pushed out of people's calendars. They may do it once or twice, but when deadlines loom it will get cut.

One way of preventing this is to establish a policy around user research. As I mentioned earlier, the UK Government Digital Service has a great policy for dealing with this. It states that if somebody hasn't spent time with a user in the last six weeks, they lose the right to be a stakeholder in any digital service. In other words, they have no say over any user-centric project if they don't spend regular time with users.

Establishing this kind of policy may seem out of reach today. But as awareness of user experience grows, that may change, and there are some policies you can create now. You will find there are two types of policies that you wish to put in place: working policies and organisational policies. Working policies are something you can establish now.

WORKING POLICIES

Working policies affect how your user experience team operates. For example, it might be policy that your team does not undertake new work without a written specification. Another policy might be that all work needs an executive sponsor to provide approval before work can be started.

The advantage of a working policy is that it rarely needs approval from outside the team. You are just defining the way you do your own job and telling others of this process in the form of a policy. As a result, you can start creating working policies today.

Unfortunately, because they are policies defined only by your team, they carry less weight. That said, having a set of working policies lets your colleagues know that you are not singling them out. As management begin to embrace user experience, encourage them to start creating company-wide policies.

ORGANISATIONAL POLICIES

An organisational policy applies to the whole organisation. Typical examples of organisational policies would include:

- Social media policy
- Accessibility policy
- Content style guide

These are policies that all colleagues have to adhere to and so they need a more formal approval process. This means getting agreement from key stakeholders (such as departmental heads) for the policy and its enforcement. Although this is not always an easy process, it is preferable to debating things on a case-by-case basis.

The great thing about organisational policies is that once approved they have real power. This means they are easier to enforce than working policies. Furthermore, people like to be consistent. If they approved a policy they are less likely to challenge it in the future.

A solid set of policies will start to reshape the culture of your organisation. But their potential has limits unless you also redefine the metrics by which you measure success.

Establish new metrics at every level

I had been working with a company for a while, guiding them through the process of digital transformation. One day they asked me to present at a company-wide away day.

The focus of my presentation was on how to make the organisation more agile. I told the story of when I attempted to launch a blog within the organisation. It took weeks for the IT team to approve the blogging platform as they needed to assess the security risks. The point I was trying to make was that the organisation was so risk-averse that it was hampering their operation.

After my talk a rather irate woman (let's call her Gill) came storming up to me. Gill was red in the face and angry. "I was the one who blocked your blog and with good reason," she said. "If a terrorist organisation hacked the website it would have reflected badly on us."

This was not a particularly high-profile organisation. What is more, many large organisations used the platform. Yes, it was possible that somebody could hack the platform, but it was unlikely. Yet in Gill's eyes it wasn't a risk worth taking.

From an organisational perspective this made no sense. But no matter how frustrating I found the experience, I did not blame Gill. You see, from her perspective, the risk was high. That is because she felt assessed on how secure the platforms were.

If the organisation failed to launch a blog it did not reflect on her. But if that blog was later hacked she would be out of a job.

The problem was that her key metric was security. She was assessed on how secure she kept the organisation and that was all. This is a common problem. When management assess people based on one criterion, it will be this criterion they worry about above all else.

This is why it is important to make it clear to staff that their responsibility is to provide a great user experience. This needs to become the main metric if you want a customer-centric culture. If you do not, people will look inwards and focus on their own role and job security. This problem is not just isolated to individual employees. I often see it at a departmental level as well. Senior management teams set departmental targets and middle management have to meet them. It is not surprising, then, when managers focus on these targets at the cost of everything else.

I worked with a marketing department whose management assessed them on the number of leads they generated. They destroyed the user experience with intrusive ways of getting visitors' email addresses.

But they did not just damage the user experience. They also flooded the sales team with low quality leads that they had to follow up. By assessing the marketing department on a single metric, senior management caused chaos.

That is the problem with metrics and assessment criteria. If you give a department or an individual a criterion by which you assess them, they will focus on that at the detriment of everything else.

Management must be careful if they are going to have departmental or individual assessment criteria. They must avoid focusing on a single metric, and instead have a number that balance one another. In particular, they must make sure there are user experience metrics in the mix.

One example is the net promoter score I mentioned back in chapter 1. This is a simple metric that applies at a company-wide or departmental level, and it focuses everybody on customer satisfaction.

Digital services should also have metrics that they need to deliver, although delivering on these metrics shouldn't be the responsibility just of the digital team: it should be the responsibility of all stakeholders across departments. That will ensure everybody focuses on making the project a success.

What these metrics are will depend on the service. A good one I use a lot is the time to complete a task. As I have said before, saving the user time is the single best thing you can do to improve the user experience. It makes sense to focus on this metric when building digital services.

Whatever metric management settle on, it is important to not obsess over it. Any metric, no matter how good, will distort organisational thinking if too much emphasis is placed on it. Key performance indicators are a guide of success, not a target with consequences if not met. It is good to have targets, but not if the cost of failure is too high.

As we know, a fear of failure can be one of the biggest barriers to building a user experience culture. A user experience culture is one where experimentation flourishes. But what else should it include? What does a user-centric business look like? As we draw to a close, I want to leave you with a picture of what your organisation should be aiming for in the long term.

A Vision Of A UX-Focused Company

I will be honest. You have a long road ahead. Changing an organisation's culture is a major undertaking. It will take years and you might not see the end. But it is a journey worth making.

It won't just help the business. It will help you too. It will develop your skills and increase your employability. It will raise your profile in the business. Most of all, it will make a tangible difference here and now. Although some of what I have written about will take years to achieve, you can apply much of what I have covered today, things that will make a difference immediately.

You can start seeking out allies today. You can establish a vision and design principles today. You can start promoting the benefits of user-centric design and raising the profile of users. None of this needs to wait and it will make an immediate difference. You can even put in place your own working policies and build an initial proof of concept.

I would encourage you to always keep your eyes on the finish line, that vision of a user-centric organisation. This will ensure you always head in the right direction. But more than that, it will remind you what you are fighting to achieve. It will remind you that there is a better way.

There is a new generation of user-centric companies that are transforming their sectors; companies which start by addressing a user need, not selling a product. Imagine what it would be like to work in a place that took the time to understand their customers' pain points, a company that took those pain points and designed products to address them. Imagine how much easier it would be to sell a product people needed!

But great user experience companies don't stop there. They are always engaging with their customers. They learn from them so that the company can improve, and they mobilise them so that their customers become their greatest advocates.

One day you will work in a company that doesn't need to pour money into traditional marketing: your customers will be promoting your products for you. A company where you are no longer firefighting PR disasters: you will instead watch your customers form communities around your brand. A place where continual iteration and experimentation is commonplace, where by monitoring user behaviour you can adapt your digital services to remain one step ahead of the competition. A culture which takes for granted continual investment in improving the user experience. One where finite digital projects are a thing of the past.

The day will come when you will no longer need to champion the user. You will not have to endlessly repeat mantras such as 'Design with data' or 'Test and iterate'. At first, you will begin to notice others saying them instead. In time, they will become embedded in the culture of the organisation. Everybody will consider the user experience, and customer satisfaction will become the key metric. Management will integrate user experience professionals across every part of the organisation. People will work seamlessly together across business silos.

Management will also become advocates of the user. They will no longer just pay lip service to customer experience; they will integrate it into the heart of organisational strategy. Most of all, they will spend regular time with customers, seeking to better understand their needs.

All this may seem like a pipe dream right now. But it is possible! It is a marathon, not a sprint, but organisations can change. They will have to change. The marketplace is on your side. Customers are demanding a better experience and those who fail to adapt will die.

The key is to take the process one step at a time, to start small and not get overwhelmed by the scale of the task. Most importanty, don't do it alone. Find like-minded colleagues and start talking. Take the time to meet others passionate about user experience outside your company. Attend conferences, reach out online, get in touch with me. I would love to hear from you! In short, find yourself a support network.

It will be demoralising at times. You will face setbacks and people who do not understand. It will be frustrating and you will make mistakes. But you can succeed. As one of my favourite quotes says:

> "*Success is going from failure to failure with no loss of enthusiasm.*"

Copyright Information

IMAGE CREDITS: